The Missing Heart
of Europe

*Does Britain hold the key to
the future of the Continent?*

by

THOMAS KREMER

with a foreword by

FREDERIC RAPHAEL

The June Press

First published in 2004

by The June Press Ltd

UK distributor
The June Press Ltd
PO Box 119
Totnes
Devon TQ9 7WA
Tel: 44(0)1548 821402
Fax: 44(0)1548 821574
Email: info@junepress.com
Web: www.junepress.com

ISBN 0 9534 6973 5

Cover design by Alice Leach

This book is printed on environmentally friendly paper
Printed in Great Britain by Kingfisher Print, Devon

For Alison who helped to make this country my home. For Jack and Sam, my two grandsons, whose lives will be shaped by the crucial decisions this nation is about to make.

Contents

Acknowledgements

In writing this book I had help and encouragement from a great many people. Most significantly, Lord David Owen was first to suggest that I put pen to paper, read and critiqued the first draft. Janet Bush sourced the material relating to the economic aspects of the Euro and was hugely supportive throughout the work. John Wakefield made some useful suggestions anent the structure of the work. In acquainting myself with Roman and Common Law, Professor Andrew Lewis pointed me in the right direction as well as saving my blushes at some elementary errors in the manuscript even though he does not wholeheartedly share my take on the subject. Judge Dr Franz-Benno Delonge guided me through the intracacies of Bavarian judiciary practices. David Lascelles had a major input relating to all matters financial and acted as a very sound sounding board all along. Discussions with Professor Silvio Yeschua contributed to the formation of the chapter on Language. Above all, without the superb editing of Roger Hudson the book would not be half as fluent and readable as it is.

Foreword

My acquaintanceship with Tom Kremer is of the slimmest variety. We may have played football together a few times in the twice-weekly pick-up games which took place in Hyde Park during the 1960s. It was one of the charms of these games that people came from all directions (Italians, Cypriots, Yugoslavs, Scots) and, as they used to say, from all walks of life (waiters, postmen, comedians, even writers). Loyalties were recruited randomly (by whichever side was a man short), but they were then fiercely engaged, until the game ended. We had no kit, no referee and the goals were between heaped coats. There were no lines on the pitch and all decisions were communally agreed, rarely with any dissent.

These games testified, in their limited way, to the capacity of disparate people to observe rules which were never exactly spelt out and to act in conformity with what Montesquieu, in a grander context, called "*the spirit of the laws*". Those who took the game too seriously, or expected deference to their fame and status (Peter Cook, for instance), rarely returned to hack another day.

When asked to write this foreword, I had no idea who Tom Kremer was, or what he did, apart from playing football. I know now, from his text, only that he was born a Transylvanian Jew, is a successful game inventor and businessman, and has lived for at least fifty years in England. He now feels himself to be British, and is certainly a patriot when it comes to our institutions and unwritten laws. He has the fervour for Britain which converts have for new faiths, but lacks the aggressive certainties which mark the bigot or the fanatic.

The strength of his arguments, for abstaining from any irrevocable commitment to much more than a European free trade zone, lies in the fact that they are neither monotonously polemic nor tiresomely equivocal. He has the dispassionate urgency and clarity of vision, which the intelligentsia of the Greek cities of Asia Minor had in the 6th and 5th centuries BC: like Thales and Herodotus, who were Hellenes with wide knowledge of the Persian barbarians, Kremer has experience of both eastern and western Europe, as he does of both sides of the Channel. He knows very well which he prefers, and for good reasons, but he has travelled widely and admires much of what he nevertheless warns us is alien to British traditions of *piecemeal social engineering*, as advocated by Karl Popper in his seminal post-war work, "The Open Society and its Enemies". The Open Society proceeds by debate, compromise and general assent; the Closed Society has an ideological agenda, and a pre-determined social structure and a *dirigiste* ruling class reinforced by a repressive *apparat*.

Kremer does not, of course, pretend that any of the states of the European Union are unreservedly of the second kind, but he does note that the histories of, in particular, Germany and France, our two principal "partners", cast a long shadow on their social habits and responses. The European Community is one more attempt, noble in conception, political in execution, which affects to start history yet again at a fanciful Day One.

Even in democracies there are significantly different ways of doing things. British justice is founded on the Common Law, in which various precedents rather than a single inflexible "text" inform and inflect what goes on in courts where the judiciary is not a function of the government. Presumed innocence is a key feature in Britain, whereas the French have a system of "investigating magistrates" whose arbitrary findings - based often on the principle of *intime conviction* (i.e. a reasoned hunch) - it is the business of the defence to disprove. There is no necessary superiority in one method rather than the other, but they remain radically different and no amount of massage will reconcile them, any more than it will the empirical traditions of British philosophy, the *a priori* system-building of the Germans and the euphonious elaborations of French metaphysics.

Although Kremer does not mince his words, he delivers his arguments with little stridency. He loves the Old Continent, but he loves it for its diversity and is alarmed by the attempt, made copiously manifest in Valéry Giscard d'Estaing's draft constitution, to impose factitious uniformities. Giscard's idealistic vision is decreed from above by a man with an *intime conviction* that he knows for certain what the peoples of Europe yearn to have (a federal state with a single taxation and foreign policy), without wondering for a moment whether those concerned should have any direct say in decisions about what is good for them.

Kremer's key insight is between "concentric" and "eccentric" states. In this he introduces a telling distinction between one style of Open Society and another, while never suggesting that today's Germany and France are not democracies. The concentric state is governed by neo-Jacobins who concentrate power at the centre or by reformed authoritarians whose citizens - the Germans for clear instance - expect orders from above. The eccentrics, exemplified by the British, but including the Dutch and Scandinavians, are used to a society unbraced by bureaucratic rigidity and delay. In the latter, as in Perikles' Athens, the citizens engage in a multiplicity of activities and enterprises, all of which contribute to the quality of life and the prosperity of the state without being supervised by it.

Giscard's draft of the European constitution - with its affectations of Holy Writ, or even of Tablets of Stone, in embryo - arouses Kremer's meticulous suspicion. He takes us through a good few of the clauses of what will, unless we are careful, determine Europe's future and shows us, with polemic patience, that there is much to fear in such prescriptive didacticism. As a resident alien - albeit now a British subject - with first-hand knowledge of other European societies, Kremer is urgently aware of merits in the indeterminate nature of British institutions which, by virtue of not belonging to any overall written scheme, are allowed both to evolve and, within the limits of civility, contradict and challenge each other.

Contradictions do not embarrass an illogical society,

which has any number of quasi-autonomous businesses, societies, and even schools. Lack of uniformity is a mark of vitality. The twisted timber of humanity can never be comfortably suited by a system tailored with rectilinear formality. Such Procrustean schemes take for granted that one size can be made to fit all; or that all can be compelled to be of one size.

Democracy not only thrives on but demands division. As the French philosopher Alain put it "*Résistance et obéissance, voilà les deux vertus du citoyen. Par l'observation, il assure l'ordre, par la résistance, il assure la liberté*". It might seem that we have nothing to fear from a French tradition which produces such a limpid expression of the need both to conform and to dissent. But would Alain have bothered to write it, had it been a truism? The French, in fact, associate obedience with the political Right and "resistance" with the Left.

Envy and emulation work together in the national psyches of, in particular, France and Germany: the former is more ashamed than grateful of American aid both during and after the war, the latter, while marginally more grateful, wishes to be done with its half-century of probation and hopes that, enveloped in a new identity, it will be allowed to regain its central authority in European affairs.

Both of the great continental powers' fears and ambitions have been too pressing for their neighbours to resist. What state that was not ashamed either by adherence to the Nazis or by its subjugation by them has eagerly embraced the submergence of its identity in the European super-state and of its fiscal independence in the Euro? The

Swiss have opted out and the Danes - whose country was uniquely uncomplicit with the Holocaust - have had grave doubts. The British, above all, lack the guilts by which Europe is riven and from which its states wish to deliver themselves by a new identity and a supposedly undifferentiated future. The extreme Euro-sceptics - among whom Kremer should not be classed - have recycled the old "foreigners begin at Calais" attitudes and affect a hermetic vanity which cannot for long suit a trading nation. Kremer advocates a free trade zone but winces, with experienced reason, at economic centralism. The British in general are rightly sceptical of grandiose rule-books and immutable formulae, especially when ordained by their continental Betters and monitored only by unsubtle vanities like those of Jack Straw and Peter Hain. Does either speak any European language with any fluency?

No ill-will or Machiavellian subterfuge need be imputed to advocates of European centralisation in order to see that they seek, above all, to homogenise, or at least confuse, the diversity of European Nations. Thus Germany will be the Gulliver at the heart of Europe, obliged to civility by the trammels of regulations and the flattery of an effusive welcome to eminence, but increasingly influential in all its policies. As for a single foreign policy, what could more certainly guarantee the highest possible quotient of humbug matched by the smallest possible disposition, or even ability, to take prompt, decisive action?

Kremer's animus is reserved for the immutable rigidities which a written constitution wishes to impose. France is, above all, a nation of *fonctionnaires*, civil servants of various stripes, from *énarques* at the top to postmen: *l'état* has a mystic quality for the French. Constitutions come and go, but *l'état* lasts forever. "The state" is to the French what "the Crown" has been for the British: something over and above the government of the day. The Germans, by contrast, have a penchant for strong men with forceful personalities who supply a centre for their concentric ambitions.

Kremer has the candour and depth of focus to portray things in a seemingly dispassionate light. He has no personal axe to grind and tells the truth as he sees it. I have learnt much from his book, often at the cost of previous assumptions and hopes. In other words, this is a book to make you think, hard.

Frederic Raphael

Introduction

The proposed European constitution, and the Euro currency, in their origin, purpose and meaning, are part of a political process that has as its objective the full integration of the continent. The French, German and British are the three dominant civilisations that have shaped the continent's recent history. Any moves towards integration hinge on how they interact. Indeed, it is difficult to envisage a rational consideration of the subject without some understanding of the key national characteristics of the people who civilised the continent.

Before embarking on what I hope is a fairly objective analysis, I have to admit to a personal bias. After the war, I had the good fortune to be given the choice to settle here and I would not, willingly, live anywhere else. I feel at ease within this society, its attitudes, values, traditions and general way of life. Whenever I return from a trip abroad I breathe easier on crossing the border. There is an air of freedom in this country that I rarely sense anywhere else. Given my chequered early life I may have oversensitive antennae but well nigh fifty years of experience on both sides of the channel tells me otherwise: there is a profound atmospheric difference between this island and the mainland.

It requires a great deal of presumption for an outsider to offer an insight to the British people who, by and large, have governed themselves better over the last few hundred years than their continental neighbours. But through accident of birth, upbringing and circumstance, I have had to familiarise myself with the languages, cultures and mindsets of the peoples who are at the heart of the current European political activity. If what I have written helps to shed some light on this great debate and bring to it an original perspective, it is due to my peculiar background that happens to span the societies at the core of the continent.

In attempting to draw some valid comparisons, it would be foolish to rank one civilisation above another. Their massive contribution to what constitutes a genuine and distinct European cultural identity is beyond dispute. But this identity was neither created nor fostered by political harmonisation or standardisation of any kind. On the contrary, the source of this rich and magnificent cultural edifice lies in a diversity of independent centres of civilisation influencing each other whilst retaining their own effective decision-making powers. In the context of integration, what we need to consider are those specific qualities that are fundamental to each civilisation, those qualities that make the French be French, the Germans be German and the British be what they are. For it is these national traits that both determine, and are determined by, the history, language, law, social custom, mindset and political culture of any given people. Whatever treaties, conventions or constitutions politicians cobble together, at the end of the day, the viability of a united Europe rests on the support and cohesion of her diverse people.

The British, not unreasonably, consider themselves normal. Seen from the mainland, however, they are eccentric. Driving on the left, jaywalking with gay abandon, hanging on grimly to awkward imperial measures two hundred years after Napoleon introduced a metric system of logical simplicity, communicating in a language virtually devoid of grammar and pronounced as it is not written, are some of the more obvious signs of this eccentricity. So are train spotting, the absence of a written constitution, amateur magistrates, the common law, habeas corpus, a trial system designed not to uncover the truth but to present a jousting contest between the protagonists of two competing, irreconcilable alternatives, idiosyncratic sentencing by ancient judges and self perpetuating, autonomous institutions like Oxford and Cambridge and the BBC that are controlled neither directly by the state nor by private enterprise. Outstanding leaders like Pitt and Churchill are dismissed at the moment of their greatest triumph, defeats and victories are studied in equal measure, people are unnaturally calm in face of disasters, congenitally unsystematic, seldom prepared, remarkably casual, while an irreverent sense of humour invades each nook and cranny of everyday life. None of this, or anything like it, pertains to the French or the Germans, nor indeed to any other nation in Europe.

At first sight, the "oddities" of this island may appear random, quirky, superficial products of historical accident. Not so. A closer look at the origins and development of the English language, at the evolution of Britain as an imperial power, at British political and legal institutions, at social and business mores, at what is instinctively understood, but not easily defined, as the British way of life, reveals a common thread running through them all.

The root of the word "eccentric" literally means "tending out of, or away from, a centre". It is the diametric opposite of "concentric" that is "tending towards a centre". This distinction, once fully grasped, goes a long way towards explaining a continental rift that led to profound, and often unfortunate, misunderstandings. We are all familiar with German habits of strict adherence to rules and regulations, of conformity; we all admire their organisational skills, efficient teamwork and systematic approach to the task in hand. We are also aware of the powerful German drive for unity, her people's instinctive deference to superior authority and need to be led by strong, autocratic leaders. Despite crucial differences between the Gallic and Teutonic temperament, the French have also always been essentially centrist in outlook, political culture and institutional life. They may resent central authority but this entrenched tendency has been strong enough to survive periodic revolutions. A clear demonstration of what is meant by the "centrist" tendency is the Brussels administration set up on the French model, in codes written in the French language by the elite French bureaucracy.

Although not as extreme as Japan where conformity is the very condition of survival, France and Germany are essentially concentric in that all significant movement radiates from a centre that commands convergence and dominates its constituent elements. Appropriately, at the end of World War Two the constitution of the German Federal Republic was contrived by the Allies in clear recognition of this attribute with the precise objective of weakening the power of the centre.

In contrast, the British are intrinsically eccentric in every aspect of their communal life. Power is more widely shared throughout society, its sources are diffuse, the centre itself, despite recent Thatcherite and Blairite tendencies, is less than monolithic. The value placed on individual rights and liberties, on the diversity of personal choice, on invention, enterprise and spontaneity, the tolerance of nonconformity and an attitude of irreverence towards external authority, are all hallmarks of an eccentric society.

Why is such an analysis, tracing fundamental distinctions between European nations germane to the debate of European integration? How does it help to inform when considering the constitution-in-the-making or the decision on joining the Euro? In the first place, the political prospects of a Greater Europe will be determined as much by the differences in mindset and culture of its diverse nations as by the common ground they share. Secondly, European history might have taken an altogether different course if British politicians had not misjudged the character of powerful continental figures like Napoleon, the Kaiser, Hitler and de Gaulle and not ignored the political cultures of the peoples dominated by them. The same, of course, is true in reverse. There has never been a true comprehension of Britain, her people and their values, on the continent. It would be tragic to repeat old mistakes and attempt to construct a common European ideal built on mutual misconceptions. Thirdly, any civilisation functions best when in harmony with its own natural tendencies. Both concentric and eccentric societies operate within political frameworks created by their specific history. The attempt to force an eccentric society, like the British, into an alien, concentric structure, would have devastating consequences.

Lastly, such an analysis may yield a surprising insight: it is possible that parliamentary democracy having its origins here, on this island, was not just a historical accident, that it had something to do with the inherent attitude of an eccentric people.

For Europe the 20th-century has been a calamity. Several hundred years of uninterrupted world domination in terms of military power, political dominion, economy, technology and culture have come to an end. The centre of the world has simply shifted elsewhere. In the First World War the leading European nations lost a generation of perhaps their finest youths. In the Second many centres of European civilisation were reduced to rubble, almost the entire population of the continent was sucked into five years of extreme hardship with significant loss of life, freedom and human dignity. The rise of fascism, the Spanish civil war, communism, the Gulags, the emergence of totalitarian regimes, the Holocaust, have all combined to shake Europe's moral, political and social foundations. What had been once considered civilised norms no longer seemed to apply. Both great wars that shaped the last century were the offspring of Europe alone. The conflagration may have enveloped most of the world, but the fire started right here. It may be justly said that Europe brought her decline upon herself.

In the aftermath of the Second World War the people of Europe began to examine what went so horribly wrong with their continent and turned their thoughts to preventing future calamities of a similar kind. The vastly altered circumstances provided the perfect soil for ideas about bringing the different nations of Europe closer together, breaking down barriers between them, creating a more harmonious continent, and establishing ideal conditions for an enduring peace.

INTRODUCTION

The lofty vision of a strife-free, seamless continent, with its diverse people living in harmony under a single unified democratic administration, irrespective of language, nationality, religion, sex, age, culture, ethnic origin, is highly seductive. However, in attempting to translate this vision into the hard currency of everyday life, we have to face the fact that there is a heavy price to pay. For such a process of unification entails giving up rights and powers painstakingly acquired over hundreds of years and at least a partial loss of national independence. It also means for all of us profound changes in our way of life.

What has been achieved by way of integration is by no means inconsiderable. We have today free movement of people, goods and capital throughout the EU; we have a common agricultural and fisheries policy; we have supranational rules governing free trade and competition; we have a European Charter of Rights and a European Court of Justice; we have a measure of common social standards and regulations affecting the workplace; we have common competition laws; we have an elected European Parliament and, not least, we have created the European Commission, a major centre of political power in Brussels. The process of integration, thus far, has been relatively slow and gradual. At each summit, and with every new treaty, the specific powers transferred to Brussels have been limited in scope and, taken individually, perhaps tolerable. The economic gains afforded by a vastly enlarged common market may have provided meaningful compensation for considerable political sacrifices.

The advent of the Euro, the suppression of national currencies, the creation of an European Central Bank to supersede the national bank of each state, the emergence of a sovereign constitution, brings the process of integration to an altogether different pitch and adds a whole new dimension to the changing political landscape of the continent. These drastic moves were bound to evoke a strong grass root reaction and deepen the divide in Britain between two warring camps. Europe has now preoccupied the political life of this country for decades. The intensity of public debate on the subject ebbs and flows with the rhythm of election cycles and the emergence of more sensational events. Yet, overall, arguments about Britain's relationship to Europe so far have been fragmented, shallow, poorly informed, inspired by party politics, sound bites and media hype. They have generated more heat than light.

Mainstream Britain has, on the whole, sound political instincts and is well disposed towards her European neighbours. The people are, at the same time, somewhat confused, bored and intimidated by the seemingly unending, and largely repetitive, stream of words engulfing the subject. Many admit openly that the complexities involved are beyond them and they would be relieved to leave the final decisions to the government of the day and their "expert" advisors. For someone like me, who was born and bred on the continent, who made his home here and has learnt over the last fifty years to appreciate what is so unique and so valuable in the British way of life, this state of affairs is deeply disturbing. For although the ultimate decision will have little impact on my own life, it may make all the difference to the lives of my children and even more so to those of my grandchildren. What I write here is addressed principally to their generation for I believe they face a danger of which they are sublimely unaware.

The threat is not an obvious one. It is not posed by the Vikings, the Armada, Napoleonic or German armies intent on invading these shores. It is subtle, insidious and more difficult to counter because it comes from within the country, as well as from the outside. The British people are being asked by their own political leaders to weaken, or even surrender those very rights, decision making powers, institutions, laws, self governing habits that alone can guarantee a degree of individual freedom enjoyed by very few other nations in the world.

It is openly acknowledged even here that the Euro is primarily a political, not an economic, currency. It is also common ground that the European Constitution, if endorsed, will mean Britain losing more of her independence. The massive enlargement of the EU is now a fact. Given that all three are major steps in the building of the continent into a Greater Europe, the issue is quite clear: what is the best British response to such an ambitious concentric continental enterprise. Is it to embrace it, support it, lead it, oppose it, try to modify it, sabotage it, withdraw altogether, or what?

Any worthwhile attempt to consider this question has to touch on a wide variety of subjects: history, constitution, law, language, governing institutions, political culture, finance, economics, business practice and the communal mindset of the principal European people. At the risk of oversimplification, and lacking academic expertise in any of these subjects, what I have attempted is to bring together apparently separate strands that have a bearing on European integration into a more coherent whole. Seeing the picture in its entirety may help people, I hope, make more rational, more informed, decisions.

In making sweeping generalisations about national traits, some of my remarks may well offend the sensibilities of various people, especially those steeped in today's multi-cultural trend and political correctness. For this I apologise. My intention throughout has not been to criticise. I love the diversity of Europe and value the individuality of the peoples within this wonderful continent. Having lived through the war, the last fifty years of almost perfect peace, the rapprochement of erstwhile enemies, the ease of moving and working across Europe, seems still a near miracle to me. A continent at peace with herself, with nations in close economic collaboration is a magnificent achievement. The threat to what has been achieved lies not in a supposed natural enmity between her diverse people. It lies, as it always has, in an over ambitious accumulation of concentric political power, be that in Madrid, Paris, Berlin, Moscow or Brussels. What should concern us all is not the establishment of a successful super state, for that will never happen, but a failed drive towards an unattainable ideal, leaving Europe, as always after such failures, in political ruins. There is just a possibility that the European peoples, left to themselves, will eventually evolve their own communal administrative structures. We must not allow visionary politicians to jeopardise that chance.

There has been much talk recently of the need for Britain to be engaged in Europe. This is plain nonsense. Since the Middle Ages, she has never been disengaged from the continent. Through trade, war, alliance and coalitions, Britain has always formed an integral part of Europe, both influencing, and influenced by, the powers of the mainland. British and European politics can only be understood within the context of a shared history. We would certainly be looking at quite a different Europe today had Britain not played such a decisive role in continental affairs since the days of Louis XIV onwards to the end of the Cold War.

What distinguishes Britain's engagement, as against those of other major players, is a consistent, long term, resistance to any emerging concentric power aimed at dominating the entire continent. Britain may in her time have accumulated an overseas empire but such a consistent support of the smaller countries against central hegemony in Europe can only be explained in terms of a deep, instinctive distrust of overbearing, centralised political structures. In a fast-changing world, Britain has a vital contribution to make in guiding the political destiny of Europe. But she can only do so if she remains true to her eccentric self.

1

A Sense of Belonging

To betray, you must first belong
Kim Philby

A nation state is composed of people who believe they are part of the same nation and share a sense of national identity. They are willing to accept the same authority because they *feel* they belong together. Generally speaking, such a sense of belonging evolves organically over a long historic period. It is this sense of belonging that unified Italy and Germany in the 19th-century and its lack broke apart Yugoslavia a few years ago. The fate of an integrated Greater Europe hinges on just this question: in the last analysis do the diverse people feel themselves to be British, French, German, Italian or European? Do they feel more at home being governed from London, Paris, Berlin or Rome or from some sort of a neutral city in a foreign land?

There is, of course, more than one sense of belonging. We belong to a village, a neighbourhood, a county, a state, and ultimately to the human race. In political terms, as long as one of them has a superior claim, there is no conflict between them. Only if, for example, one feels as strongly about the world-wide proletariat or about Islam as about one's own country, can there be a difficulty. Unless the integrationists force the issue, a national sense of identity may live happily side by side with a feeling of being a European. In fact, resisting the process of integration makes it easier, not more difficult, to identify with the continent.

Nation states, currently the principal political structures, may not last forever. We may envisage, sometime in the distant future, a unified global government seated on a planet somewhere in our galaxy with fellowship of the human race being the dominant sense of belonging. It is difficult to conceive, however, such a state of affairs coming into being as a result of clever manoeuvring by a few politicians.

To have a government in Edinburgh is possible because the Scots have a sense of national identity. Whether it becomes the government of an independent Scotland or shrinks into relative impotence depends entirely on the strength of the sense of belonging of the Scottish people. To divide England into five or six regional governments will never work since there are hardly any individuals on this island calling themselves North Westerners or South Easterners or whatever artificial name any such arbitrary area happens to be given. There is no conceivable reason why the people of Truro should feel more at home being governed from Bristol than from London. Like the Dome, without coherent content, they will turn out to be an expensive failure and vanish, sooner rather than later, into administrative oblivion.

Since it is fairly obvious that no one can successfully govern people from a political centre to which the people feel they do not belong, the architects of a Greater Europe set about trying to change national sentiment. The replacement of national currencies by the Euro, the drafting of a sovereign European constitution, the wholesale transfer of decision-making powers from the nation states to the European Union, the establishing of a powerful central authority in Brussels, are all moves that, in their totality, are expected by the integrationists to make people consider themselves more European and consequently less nationalistic. Except in the UK, this is not a hidden agenda, although politicians are always clever enough to fudge the issue of double loyalties. So, for example, Helmut Kohl would declaim with pride: "My home is Germany, my future is Europe".

For anyone living outside the hothouse of daily politics, it may be difficult to envisage how a national sense of belonging that was centuries in the making, can be instantly fabricated, transplanted, or imposed by a series of political interventions. What makes a Frenchman feel French, a German feel German, is the sum total of an ethnic and environmental heritage that goes back countless generations, and has little to do with contemporary politics. History makes it abundantly clear that it is this sense of belonging, the sense of national identity, that draws the political boundaries and not the other way around. This is as true of Europe as anywhere else, as true now as it has ever been. Europe is a distinct geographical and cultural entity. She has a rich history of her own. Her inhabitants do consider themselves to be Europeans. The question is how does this translate into a common political future, a future compatible with her existing and diverse nation states. And the answers to it will shape the future of the continent and its people for the remainder of this century.

To be at the heart of Europe, to play a key role in Europe, to lead Europe, and other similar sound bites are constantly on the lips of pro-Euro politicians, the last two Prime Ministers prominent among them. Corollary phrases, such as, *Britain will be marginalized, Britain will be excluded from the core, Britain will lose her political clout, Britain will be left behind,* sound dire warnings and are intended to frighten the people of Britain into ever closer political union with the continent. Political leaders in this country seem to have an omnipresent daydream and a recurrent nightmare. In the daydream they travel the world as representatives of a European superpower, meet their American, Russian and Chinese counterparts on at least equal terms and settle gigantic political issues on a global scale. In the nightmare scenario they sit, in the company of Swedish and Danish colleagues, on smallish stools in a sort of cramped antechamber, whilst the leaders of Portugal, Greece, Luxemburg and the other Euro countries are comfortably ensconced in the magnificence of the adjoining conference hall. The door between the antechamber and the hall is closed. From time to time, however, a Kafkaesque messenger emerges to inform the three hapless men of momentous decisions reached in their absence.

It may be interesting to discover first where the heart of this ancient continent beats. Is it in Brussels, in the administrative body of the European Union? Is it in Strasbourg, in a parliament elected by a tiny percentage of the population, too feeble to significantly influence events? Does it wander from summit to summit? Does it bleed in bilateral confrontations between leaders fighting for their national priorities? Does it supply the lifeblood of multilateral bargaining that results in abstract, fudged compromises? It is pertinent to ask these questions since leading politicians of all nations labour under the misapprehension that it is they who are actually shaping the future of Europe. Absorbed in feverish deals, drafting impressive declarations, passing hard-fought, carefully crafted resolutions, they suffer the illusion that the outcome of political negotiations will translate itself into an ultimate reality that resembles their intentions. If there is one thing that history teaches us, it is that international treaties, grand political designs, ideological constructs, have a brief life-span and seldom turn into a reality recognisable to their authors. In the context of a pan-European settlement, the Versailles deal of 1919 should serve both as lesson and warning. In Britain it is generally recognised that politics is the art of the possible. In many parts of the continent it is still believed to be that of the desirable. What affect changes in countries, nations and the lives of people, are wars, climatic conditions, natural disasters, technological advances and patterns of economic activity. Political frameworks tend to reflect profound changes, not determine them. Wise statesmen may help improve society a little, clever politicians almost invariably do it a lot of harm.

Europe does have a heart, a soul and even something of a nascent identity. This heart, this soul is not something to be cultivated in a hastily constructed political union. It is part of a shared history, of diverse cultures with strong common features, of successive layers of a rich, turbulent civilisation that rivalled even the venerable Chinese one. Homo Europaeus has not done too badly in the course of the last two millennia. It is possible to think of this civilisation beyond its art, architecture, music, literature, education, science and shared ethical values. There is a sense of familiarity, of instinctive understanding, of mental proximity between the peoples within the continent that does not encompass Asia, Africa or the Americas. In Britain, with her Anglo-Saxon culture, language and Commonwealth relations, this sense may not be quite as palpable, but it is real and distinct in the rest of Europe. Crossing the now virtually unmanned Belgian or Dutch or German borders with some nonchalance is quite a different experience from flying off to Amman, Peking, Bulawayo or Kansas City. And it is not just a matter of physical distance.

It is this communal sense that inspired the natural emergence of cross-border bodies in all spheres of activity: commerce, industry, science and the professions. Institutions to coordinate coal and steel production, to carry out atomic particle research, to establish a pan-European patent law, to build the Concorde, grew out of practical need and a shared desire to create better alternatives. What characterised these moves was that they were neither initiated nor imposed by a central political authority. Critically, they did not forcibly replace existing national structures. Thus, it is still open for me, as an inventor, to obtain a separate patent for each individual European country, though it is easier and less expensive to obtain the same protection through a single Europe-wide patent. The exact opposite holds true of the Euro: it is centrally imposed and it is a replacement, not an alternative.

Despite all the instincts of national self-preservation, there has been every indication that the peoples of this continent are ready to cross boundaries and come closer together in an organic and gradual process. Why has this not happened before and what is there to hinder such a movement now? Whilst Europe was the centre of the modern world, political leaders of nation states could indulge in what they saw as their God-given mission to compete and enlarge their territorial dominion within the continent. Although the French and the Germans may not be the best of friends, there is no evidence of a visceral hatred between the two nations strong enough to combust spontaneously into a full-scale war. Such hatreds are usually the residues of wars, not the prime causes of them. Over the last two centuries it was not popular sentiment but governments that initiated wars, and concentric governments at that. It is a lot easier to go to war if there is no need to consult people and ask parliaments to approve its attendant costs. Genuine democracies do not like to march to martial tunes, and thus are invariably disadvantaged at the start of every armed conflict.

In economic, military and cultural terms, Europe is no longer the undisputed centre of planet Earth. With the focus shifting to the United States and the Far East, the nations of this continent have a historic opportunity, almost an imperative, to draw closer together, to ally themselves in face of forces, more numerous or technically superior or better resourced or simply hungrier, elsewhere in the world. This coming together, if it is to work, has to be an alliance, a binding association entered into freely and willingly by nations confident of retaining their individual identity. Such an association is only possible among peoples who are in the habit of participating in the decision-making process, who are used to ruling themselves, who favour an eccentric form of government.

For Europe to become a coherent continent, the man in the street has to feel a sense of belonging, has to identify with a larger community, has to respect the representatives he elects, has to believe that his voice counts for something. The stream of directives from Brussels regulating life more and more, the irrelevance of the MEPs, the unaccountability of EU commissioners and the cynical bartering at summits, make all this impossible. The political establishments of the concentric countries, like France and Germany, have already alienated their own electorates to a dangerous degree and even in Britain, due to the more presidential style of government of recent years, people feel politically sidelined. What credibility can attach to the un-elected leaders and a motley crowd of remote officials entrusted with conducting the affairs of over 400 million people in Brussels?

The overt intention of Greater Europe idealists is to reconcile peoples and protect citizens. Yet every integrationist move to extend and strengthen central authority over the continent erodes the independence of nations and curtails the freedom of the individual. It cannot be otherwise. You cannot win hearts by torrents of restrictive legislation, by removing effective elective powers, by setting up manifold layers of controls, each one ever more remote. You do not gain the long-term support of people by high-level political machinations, by setting up central bodies, by creating currencies, writing constitutions, squabbling over subsidies, scrambling for the top job. Every addition and modification to existing treaties provides further opportunities for national conflict. Every piece of new legislation adds to the burden of an already over-regulated society. Every congress of political leaders, be it summit, convention, bi-lateral or multi-lateral horse-trading session, merely helps to foster hostility in the common man towards the existing European Union. Deals struck behind closed doors between a German Chancellor and a French President to settle key issues which are then presented as a *fait accompli* to the rest of the EU, are not going to delay a European convergence, they will kill it stone dead.

It is a paradox, but should not be a surprise, to find that the same political forces that kept nationalist flames burning bright in the past, now form the greatest single obstacle to a slow but enduring rapprochement of the European nations. What started initially as a popular yearning for a peaceful continent and led to the formation of a modest and useful Common Market, has been hijacked by leaders steeped in a concentric tradition for the creation of yet another grandiose political project. In contrast, the late-mediaeval north German Hanseatic League and the United States serve as useful examples of integrations that really worked. In both cases, there was a strong drive from the grass roots, a common purpose clearly understood by the people involved, a willingness to contribute to the common cause, not just grab all the benefits going. They developed not merely with the consent of the constituent elements but also with their active support. Such a groundswell of enthusiasm, noticeable in the early days of the Common Market, has now disappeared in a miasma of concentric politics, even in the mainland of Europe.

The choice facing the people of this country is not one of alternative currencies or constitutions, it is one of alternative political futures: either embracing a movement towards a federalist Europe or preserving an essentially British way of political life. Joining the Euro-zone or adopting a sovereign European constitution clearly is a watershed. The issue is not one of abstract forms of words or the convenience of exchanging money abroad or even of gaining some putative economic advantages in an uncertain future. The issue is the status of Britain in the context of a fully integrated continent, her independence, her economic well being, her security, her foreign policy and international influence. At stake are the rights and liberties of the individual so freely enjoyed by everyone on these islands, rights and liberties long in the forging but now taken for granted by post war generations.

But is a fully integrated, united, Greater Europe a realistic prospect and ought Britain to join the attempt to bring it about? This question in turn raises a host of others: Who are the people who will govern it? What are the political traditions that will nourish it? What is the track record of the continental nation states that form its membership? What is the political culture in which they are wont to operate? Where is to be the centre from which such a huge federation is to be governed? How will such a central authority cope with the diversity of disintegrating nation states? How does all this relate to British political history, culture and tradition? Is Britain likely to perform better as part of a continental mix or making her own way in the world? What does Britain stand to lose by partaking in such an ambitious enterprise? Are there other options available? Is belonging to a regional trading block incompatible with political independence?

These are fundamental questions and need some urgent answering, even if there is no referendum on the European constitution or the Euro in the immediate future. The creeping process of political integration moves relentlessly on and, like the consumption of salami, slice by thin slice, the sovereignty of nation states is being eaten away. When the number of hours an employee is permitted to work any given week is decided by a government that no longer resides in Westminster, perhaps it is time to take account.

In considering whether to accept or reject the somewhat strident invitation of an expectant, impatient Europe, it is essential to become a little more familiar with its political habits, with the history, language, laws, culture and national traits that helped to fashion the mores of so highly complex a continent. For generations, there has been a profound mutual lack of understanding on both sides of the Channel. The state of the French nation following the First World War, her lack of military will and political exhaustion was never fully grasped by the British political establishment. Nor could the mind of a man like Chamberlain, steeped in centuries of British political tradition, encompass the phenomenon of a Hitler or understand the special relationship that has always bound the German people to their leader. Hitler, on the other hand, could never comprehend to his dying day why Churchill turned down his generous offer of sharing world dominion following the defeat of France. It seemed so reasonable to him, and to most neutral observers, for Britain to retain her empire and let the unified continent of Greater Germany address the Communist threat from the East. In misreading the British character, Germany missed her chance at Dunkirk, lost the Battle of Britain and eventually the war. But that very war might have been avoided altogether had the British possessed a clearer understanding of inherent German and French national traits.

Nothing illustrates this political chasm better than the unfortunate habit shared by umpteen continental integrationists, like Jacques Delors, Joschka Fischer, Romano Prodi, of urging the British people to conform, admonishing them for their lack of political courage, warning them of the dire consequences should they not heed the universal call to European unity. Obviously they are blissfully unaware that Brits do not like being lectured by their own politicians, never mind foreign ones.

In a climate of political correctness every observation relating to national traits or cultural characteristics is highly suspect and is likely to be denounced as racist or xenophobic. Clearly, in what follows we are not comparing individual human beings. People throughout the West have nowadays comparable standards of living, similar ambitions and expectations in life, share the same concerns about the environment, listen to the same music, drive the same cars, read the same bestsellers, watch the same blockbuster movies. In this sense, there is not much to chose between a Scot, an Italian, a German, a Belgian, and so on. They are as cruel, kind, selfish, generous, responsible, negligent, stupid, intelligent, cowardly or brave as each other. What matters in this context, is where they differ in their collective persona: when they come together and function as a group, be it a village community, a business, an institution, an organisation, a nation, a body politic. The group dynamic, shaping and being shaped by a most particular history, bestows a distinct character upon the various peoples of Europe and underlie each one's unique sense of national identity.

Generalising about national traits, on one level, is a harmless pastime. Germans are thought to lack a sense of humour. The French are thought to be very fond of their food: they are definitely particular in what they eat, how it is prepared and presented. But then they have demanding standards of dress, style and language too. Italians are supposed to have close-knit families and volatile temperaments. Brits are seen as cool and casual, a characteristic useful in wartime but devastating when it comes to having a simple cooker installed. Even the more weighty matters of cultural divergences in art, literature, music and philosophy are of interest in this context only insofar as they affect the social or political attitudes and structures that distinguish a given nation.

What does matter is how a country adopts her leaders, how she allows herself to be governed, how individual people respond to authority and how authorities treat them, the stability of a nation's institutions, the foundations of her laws and the means of enforcing them: in short, her political instincts and the way she carries on the business of government. The point of such comparisons is not to pass a value judgement, to place the political culture, attitudes and institutions of one nation over that of another. It is to discover whether they are sufficiently similar, sufficiently compatible, for them to be welded into a structure that will hold. In other words, to learn what fundamental changes in national character, custom and general approach are required for the European ideal to become an enduring reality.

Such a comparative analysis is vital since in the last half century politicians right across the European spectrum have studiously ignored any mention of national divides.

Any talk of divergences focuses on transitory statistical data relating to inflation, GDP or debt, and not, for example, on the practical administration of the law that can keep a group of British plane spotters stewing in a Greek jail for over a month without being charged, or on the utter Spanish disregard for the rights and wishes of the people of Gibraltar, or the cavalier dismissal by the French and Germans of the Growth and Stability Pact that was supposed to underpin the Euro currency. These are just a few, maybe unimportant, instances highlighting differences in political culture, but they are characteristic. They also touch on democracy, supposedly one of the cornerstones of the European Union.

If all democracy means is that a state has a government elected by universal suffrage of its citizens, all member states are democratic. But then so are most countries in Africa, Asia and South America where once in every few years a great many people are seen putting crosses on bits of pre-printed paper. If we give the term a meaningful content, if we define modern democracy as a culmination of a long historical process that protects the life and dignity of the individual within the state, that devolves genuine power through layers of elected government to ordinary men, that separates the legislative and executive arms of an administration, that makes politicians and officials of all sorts individually accountable, that requires the consent of the governed and where the fourth estate, crude and overweening though it may be, has a vital part to play in political life, if it is a whole political tradition and culture that we are talking about, then indeed there are profound differences between European nations. If democracy is defined as a mindset, then German, French and British mindsets are not at all the same.

In his *Republic*, Plato examines four types of government: tyranny, oligarchy, democracy and demagogy. Finding fatal flaws in each, he rates none of them too highly. The particular weakness of democracy lies in the ease with which it tends to degenerate into demagogy. Judging by prevailing tendencies, the emphasis on the personalities, the importance of the television image, the power of sound bites and the influence of tabloids, Plato was not far off the mark. Yet, to be democratic, nowadays, equates with being good, while "undemocratic" is a pejorative term. Governments, parties and politicians all compete to appear more and more democratic. Indeed, in popular opinion no system is democratic enough. At the same time, we all know in our heart of hearts, that life is not like that. An indulgent parent, guided by children's clamour, may not necessarily be a good parent. A manager, highly sensitive to the feelings of the staff, may not necessarily be an effective manager. A minister, constantly seeking consensus, may not necessarily be a successful minister. Majority decisions are probably as often wrong as they are right. Turning points in history and advances in civilisations are mostly the result of actions of individuals taken against convention and in the teeth of public opposition.

Generally speaking, the workings of democracy are inversely proportional to the numbers involved. An Israeli kibbutz, a rural parish, permit continuous participation of individuals in the decision-making process. As we move to local government and national parliaments such participation is more and more diluted. In a supra-national Europe, even within a formal democratic framework, few individuals would feel a sense of being part of any political process. As for the over one billion inhabitants of China, despite a strong democratic instinct manifest in family groupings and smaller communities, the Western model of democracy is just not a practical option.

Britain, historically, has a deeper, more enduring, democratic tradition than that of continental nations but this by no means implies that the British political system is inherently better or that the British are morally superior to other nations. What history demonstrates is that British political culture, temperament and instinct are very different from those prevailing on the continent. Similar disparities, less pronounced perhaps, are also discernable between nations across the whole of Europe.

2

A Touch of History
- The Eccentrics

If men could learn from history, what lesson it might teach us! But passion and party blind our eyes, and the light which experience gives is a lantern on the stern, which shines only on the waves behind us
Samuel Taylor Coleridge

Does it matter why and how each nation developed its own particular form of government, now that we are all good democrats, going solemnly to polling stations every few years, enjoying free speech, basic human rights and the protection of the law? The answer to this question depends on how we expect the treaties that underpin the European Union to work.

If they are considered sacrosanct documents, signed and sealed by states of similar political cultures who will interpret them identically and are willing to abide by them in letter and spirit, who will subordinate their national interests for the common European good, then, for the purposes of the Greater Europe debate, history is irrelevant.

If, on the other hand, we look at the treaties not in abstract isolation but merely as part of the ongoing relations between living European nations, each with her own distinct political culture, her own agenda, her own approach to the status and interpretation of international treaties, her own governmental habits, then some awareness of history is vital. All the written agreements and collective European decisions are of little use when France can, and did, defy the Commission and even the Court of Justice in order to exclude British beef from her markets for a number of crucial years. In our personal and business relations we naturally take great account of past patterns of behaviour as useful guides to the future. People do change, but not many and not very often. The same is true of nations, only more so.

History is never a mere collection of facts. Any account of the past is somewhat selective, biased and tainted by the vantage point from where and when it is composed. What follows is highly selective, personally biased and written at a dramatic moment when the political map of an entire continent is being radically redrawn. Based on standard textbooks, the chosen material is intended to illustrate the very different historical paths European countries took to reach their current, similar and dissimilar, democracies. The bias derives from personal exposure to the many different political cultures across the continent. And the vantage point is, of course, selected for the light is sheds on the Greater Europe project.

Britain

Before the 16th-century fundamental divisions within the

continent ran along dynastic and feudal, rather than national lines. Latin was still the language of the intellectual establishment and the power of a Holy Mother Church crossed all secular boundaries. Allegiances were to monarchs or princes rather than sovereign territories. Patriotism, where it existed, was confined to the literary discourse of intellectuals. Europe, fragmented as it was, retained much of its mediaeval cohesiveness. By the close of the century this pattern was broken by the Reformation and the divergence of England from the trend towards absolute rule in most of Europe. Spain, France and England, each through a common native language, a unified administration by full-time government servants and a glamorised monarchy, were established political states more or less within their present boundaries. The people living within these boundaries began to feel themselves as part of a nation with all that this means. Thus Shakespeare, writing in Elizabethan England, depicts the battle of Agincourt not as an enterprise of the Plantagenet dynasty, which it was, but as a great confrontation between two nations fighting for supremacy, which it was not. *Henry V* draws not only on a strong prevailing nationalist sentiment, it also touches on cultural and linguistic differences, already perceived as national traits.

Some historians claim to detect England's nascent democratic habits in Anglo-Saxon society, others turn, less ambitiously, to the Magna Carta. Other, more tangible factors, certainly played a part. Changes in the mid 16th-century to property law made many tenants virtual freeholders. The vast tracts of land acquired by the Crown at the Dissolution of the Monasteries were soon sold by

Henry VIII to finance his extravagant wars, and not all of it fell to the nobility. As land values increased twentyfold in the next hundred years, this represented a huge transfer of wealth and of power down the social scale. No such events took place on the continent. By the end of the Elizabethan era, England had a less feudal type of aristocracy, a property-owning, vigorous middle class nourished by individual enterprise and a House of Commons powerful enough to defy, and eventually dethrone, a king just a few decades later.

The House of Commons, as its name so eloquently suggests, was nothing like its contemporary continental counterparts: occasional grand assemblies of a country's notables to formally endorse royal edicts. Being the representative body of a class that owned and controlled the greater part of the nation's wealth, the House of Commons exercised considerable influence on foreign policy, taxation and economic life in general. Wars, then as ever, were expensive. In a very inflationary age the royal revenues were quite inadequate to pay for them. From the 1580s, for example, Elizabeth was increasingly forced to have recourse to parliament to finance wars against Spain and campaigns in Ireland.

By the beginning of the 17th-century, the Crown had little coercive power and the art of governing England was one of persuasion. James I may have believed himself to be an absolute monarch, deriving his authority directly from God, but in practice he accepted that every one of his actions as king was subject to judicial review. Amazingly for a major European power, in 1630 there were fewer than 2000 paid public officials and most of them were the king's domestic servants, stable boys, cooks, gardeners, etc.

Therefore government had to be by consent. This meant not only government through an intermittent parliament, but also government by unpaid, voluntary officials throughout England. Some 10,000 or so gentry controlled the assessment and collection of taxes, the maintenance, training and deployment of the militia, the implementation of social and economic legislation and the trial of most criminals. Even senior judges were asserting their independence of the Crown with their champion, Lord Chief Justice Coke, insisting that their posts should not be forfeit at the whim of the king.

What led to the civil wars is the subject of much historical debate. Religious divides played a major part and so did the breakdown in the relationship between crown and parliament that had worked tolerably well for Elizabeth and James. Charles I certainly took the notion of the divine rights of kings a little more seriously than his father did. The whys of the civil war matter less than the event itself, for its consequences taught the nation some important lessons. First, no ruler can survive long-term without the consent of the ruled. There seem to be enough people scattered throughout the land to take the initiative and resist. Second, revolutions tend to create havoc and are followed by periods of general instability when the population is worse off than before. Third, radical political upheavals result in forms of government far from those intended by their instigators. Few parliamentarians in 1642 could have envisaged a Cromwellian dictatorship. Fourth, a government inspired by visionary ideals, as was the Protectorate by Calvinist zeal, does not do much for individual rights or civil liberties. Fifth, Englishmen emerged with an enduring suspicion of standing armies, and an antipathy towards puritanism.

Quite remarkably for an age when Louis XIV was launching his career as the greatest autocrat of them all, a freely elected parliament restored Charles II to the English throne. Louis' famous pronouncement *"L'Etat, c'est Moi"* certainly did not apply to his royal cousin. The House of Commons made a point of not restoring to the king the prerogative court of Star Chamber and the right to raise ship money, thereby removing the possibility of ruling without parliament for any length of time. When James II allowed his Catholic faith to obliterate the lessons of the previous forty years, he was smoothly replaced in the Glorious Revolution of 1688: no bloodletting, no axe or guillotine on this occasion. From the accession of William and Mary there could be no doubt that what England had created, uniquely in Europe and well ahead of anywhere else, was a parliamentary, constitutional monarchy.

The removal of the licensing of printing presses meant the effective abolition of censorship in 1695. The first daily newspaper appeared in 1702 and by 1776 there were 53 of them in London alone. Nothing vaguely comparable was to be found on the continent throughout that time. Just as important for the future social order and diversity was what has been called "The Convivial Revolution". From the 1660s and into the 18th century, voluntary societies, coffee houses, dining clubs, provincial literary and scientific societies burgeoned and gave rise, from below, to a mass of institutions that owed little to the promptings of government from above. These, in turn, ensured the autonomy of the counties which, apart from taxation and militia, and unlike their continental counterparts, were effectively free of central control. For example, the Quarter

Sessions, the chief administrative local authority, was made up of unsalaried gentry, unqualified bar property ownership.

The Toleration Act of 1689 was the first step in the formal recognition of religious pluralism and came shortly after Louis XIV had driven 400,000 protestant Huguenots out to France, many taking refuge in England. The Bill of Rights of the same year clearly circumscribed hereditary right. Monarchs henceforth owed their title to the determination of the propertied classes, precisely at the time when absolutism was in the ascendant in the rest of the continent. Even more significantly, the foundation of the Bank of England in 1694, and the bringing of the repayment of the National Debt gradually under its control, secured Westminster's central place in future constitutional development. For the channelling of private wealth into public expenditure, through the purchase of government stocks, and everything to do with the control of the land tax, as well as some other taxes, became the province of Parliament, and especially that of the House of Commons, as overseer of the Bank.

The 18th-century sees the centre of gravity shift not only from King to parliament but specifically from the House of Lords to the Commons. Robert Walpole, the dominant politician of the first half of the century, who understood the mechanics of power better than any of his contemporaries, refused as Prime Minister to be elevated to the Upper House, which illustrates this shift perfectly.

What was to become perhaps the most characteristic feature of British political life, the rivalry of two opposing parties and the periodic transfer of power from the one to the other in an orderly fashion, was now well established.

The Whigs and the Tories, as two opposing poles in a permanent political dialectic, were a truly great English invention. Despite distortions due to patronage and one-party dominance for stretches of the 18th-century, the two-party system has been more influential and endured longer than any other tradition in the political world. That Her Majesty should have a loyal, legitimate, officially recognised and funded Opposition, alongside her Government, is still considered quaint on a continent where there has never been anything like it.

All in all, despite the second Jacobite rebellion of 1745, recurrent food riots in the following decades, riotous elections in towns with a large electorate like Coventry and large-scale disturbances surrounding John Wilkes's somewhat premature campaign for greater electoral rights and full freedom of the press, the complexion of Georgian England was one of slowly growing political inclusiveness and relative stability. Dr Johnson, looking back, could observe with some justification that whereas Walpole was a "minister given by the king to the people, Pitt was a minister given by the people to the king".

In terms of foreign affairs, the century began with Marlborough's triumphs at Blenheim and Ramillies; by the end of the decisive Seven Years War (1756-1763), the British Empire had been considerably expanded. The two underlying themes of British foreign policy for the next 200 years were becoming quite clear: containment in Europe and trade-led expansion overseas. Apart from Minorca, Malta, Cyprus and the Rock of Gibraltar, serving as essential naval bases, and the Greek Ionian Islands for a brief period, England has had no territorial interests in Europe. The point of any military intervention on the continent has always been to counteract the expansion of one or other major power, be it Habsburg Spain, Bourbon or Napoleonic France, Hohenzollern or Nazi Germany, when they aspired to continental hegemony.

Although the Navy and to a lesser extent the Army, as well as outstanding generals like Clive and Wolfe, played a crucial part in helping to secure important territories, it was a host of adventurous, rugged, self motivated individuals who were the making of the Empire. As sea captains, colonisers, planters, engineers, miners, administrators and traders, they worked for themselves or within trading organisations like the British East India Company, to establish something akin to the erstwhile Venetian Empire: that is to say, a small island-based naval power with extensive overseas possessions, where military prowess and commercial drive were inextricably interwoven. In the world of religion, 18th-century individualism is manifest in a weakening Anglican Church, challenged by Presbyterians in Scotland and with Quakers, Dissenters and Methodists gaining ground everywhere. In contrast to Catholic countries, non-conformism was now already an acceptable way of life.

Society itself was changing profoundly. French visitors like Voltaire and the Abbe Grosley noticed the lack of 'caste' in the country and the ease of movement up and down the social scale. They were impressed by the relative absence of aristocratic privileges and advantages. Peers had to pay tolls at the new turnpikes and some of them, although tried in the Upper House, suffered the gallows like common criminals. The proverbial English gentleman was notoriously hard to define: a little money, a minimal dress sense, a reasonably educated manner and the right accent, were more than sufficient.

What foreign visitors saw, in sharp contrast to the Continent, was the emergence of Middle England. The substantial tenant farmer and his urban counterpart, the doctor, lawyer, business man, army or navy officer, had much in common. Often self-made, always dependent on the aggressive use of their talents, together they controlled the most dynamic portions of the economy. Politically their supremacy was seldom challenged in the larger towns and in most rural parishes. The dominant tone of this class was its pragmatic attitude and commercial logic; thus it was perfectly placed to take the leading role in the incipient Industrial Revolution. To Middle England this now added successive layers of people absorbed in manufacture and trade rising from a working class as yet unconscious of itself, moving with relative ease up the social ladder to take their share in the increasing general affluence. It was this entrepreneurial culture that enabled inventors like Arkwright with his water-powered spinning frame, James Watt with a separate-condenser steam engine, Maudsley with his screw-cutting lathe, and great civil engineers like Brindley, Smeaton, Telford and Rennie, to help Britain become the leading nation of the 19th-century.

The concept of the rule of law has always been one of the most fundamental of English traditions. No matter how partial its administration, especially in the 18th-century, it was still regarded as a common possession. No one was above the law. Not even the King. The last one who entertained doubts about this had his head chopped off. This belief not only survived the impact of industrialisation, in time it was much strengthened. Bribery and corruption in the courts started to decline, while laws enacted by parliament enhanced material progress and helped to resolve inevitable social tensions occasioned by rapid economic change.

For the origins of the Great Reform Act of 1832 one has to go back to the concerns of 1780 that George III, taking advantage of parliamentary corruption, was trying to re-establish a personal rule. Britain subsequently had its fair share of the various egalitarian movements, revolutionary idealists and forces that threatened the constitutional status quo throughout Europe, especially at the time of the French Revolution. Where she differed from most of her continental neighbours was in having a balanced form of government sensitive and flexible enough to absorb these challenges into gradual reforms, thus obviating the need for revolution. Tom Paine's book *The Rights of Man* that sold 200,000 copies in a semi-literate society, the Peterloo Massacre of 1819, the monster rallies organised by the 'Political Unions' in 1831, Chartism with its national appeal between 1838 and 1842, could all have led to radical upheaval and instant transformation of the body politic. They did not. But the pressure they generated forced the establishment to yield bit by bit and resulted in tangible, meaningful reforms. 1825 saw the repeal of anti-trade union legislation. 1829 brought Catholic Emancipation. The Great Reform Act abolished the rotten boroughs, created new constituencies in the emerging industrial centres and broadened significantly the voting franchise.

In 1848, when Marx and Engels drafted their famous manifesto and the whole continent was seething with revolution, John Stuart Mill, the quintessentially English philosopher, reconciled utilitarianism with gradual reform in his writings and was demonstrating a sympathetic attitude to moderate working-class leaders. In any case by the 1850s the British working classes were enjoying, to some degree, the protection of the law as well as cheaper food thanks to the removal of the protective corn duties in 1846. Trade unions of skilled workers learned that pressure on MPs was more effective than public demonstration. Instead of manning barricades, they became an essential part of the political process.

Unlike its continental counterparts, government never attempted to nationalise, control or mastermind the great enterprises, the infrastructure, or the financial base of the country's burgeoning industries. Free Trade and the philosophy of laissez-faire were fundamental to Victorian Britain. The protectionist Tories lost six consecutive elections fought partly on these issues between 1847 and 1868. The Tariff Reform campaign, proposing an Imperial Customs Union analogous to the German Zollverein, was decisively rejected in the spectacular collapse of the Balfour government of 1905. But free trade and *laissez-faire* went beyond abolishing protective tariffs and exemplified a political, social and economic structure in which the individual was expected to be able to stand alone. Individualism, self-respect, self-reliance, enterprise and the organisation of voluntary bodies formed the foundation of British success. The virtue of successive governments was in stepping back and just letting people get on with it.

Political reform became a continuous, organic process. The abolition in 1855 and 1861 of stamp duty on newspapers and customs duty on paper led to a massive increase of readership. Media-inspired politics and the consequent power of public opinion, perhaps a mixed blessing, reached dimensions unprecedented anywhere on the continent. The Acts of 1867 and 1884 increased the electorate from 20 per cent to 60 per cent of adult men in towns and 70 per cent in the counties, but universal suffrage had to wait till after the First World War. The Education Act of 1902 went some way to establish secondary education but as such matters had been traditionally left to the initiative of local authorities, the schools system was still patchy and much inferior to its German equivalent. On the other hand, British social reforms of the late 19th-century were, unlike those on the continent, more permissive than compulsory.

In the course of over two hundred years of European conflicts it fell to Britain to act as protector and ally of threatened, smaller nations. Turkey, Greece, Belgium, Poland, Czechoslovakia, Holland, Denmark, among others, owed their independence, at one time or other, to British arms. But the two world wars cost the nation dear. The long-term economical and political benefits were no recompense for the drain on life, resources, money and energy expended. For these, and other reasons that lie beyond Europe, the dismantling of the empire was inevitable. On the whole, this painful process was voluntary and relatively peaceful. A British-inspired form of government has taken firm root in some former colonies, for example Australia, New Zealand, Canada, India and the United States. In others, especially in Africa and the Asian sub-continent, the democratic framework survives but is, alas, bereft of content. For democracy lies not in the ritual pilgrimage to a ballot box but in the mindset of the people who know how to live by it.

The British political way of life is traditionally one where change is continuous, organic, and laboriously slow. The extension of democratic empowerment from the few to the vast majority, as voting qualifications shifted from men of title and vast property to untitled men of small property, from men of some importance to men of no importance at all, from university men to men of a bare elementary education, from men to women, took well over three hundred years. The removal of restrictions based on religion, race, occupation and class was an equally prolonged and tortuous process. Civil rights, personal liberties and free speech, now ingrained in the texture of British culture, were prized from central authority in hundreds of little uneven fragments over many, many centuries.

Despite moves under Thatcher and Blair towards a more presidential style of government, Britain's historic tendency has been for power to be decentralised, for society to become more politically active and inclusive. The corollary of such a tendency is to value the individual at least as highly as the state: the inspiration, initiative and drive for social, economic and political change originates with individuals or groups of individuals, not with central authority. Thus developments are spontaneous, episodic, unplanned and pragmatic, definitely not part of a grand central design or guided by a written constitution. These are the defining qualities of a typically eccentric society, of an eccentric political culture. Its opposite, the concentric society and culture, tends to centralise power, to place the state above the individual, to systematise, to plan on a large scale and effect changes with radical immediacy. To put the difference at its simplest, in eccentric cultures changes are from the bottom up, in concentric cultures they are from the top down.

The Netherlands

The first seventy years of what might be termed the Dutch nation state, from the Union of Utrecht in 1579 to the Treaty of Munster in 1648, were spent in a bitter, bloody and well-nigh continuous struggle for independence from a rigorously Catholic, autocratic Spain. Of course, nascent democratic instincts are discernible already centuries earlier, given the municipal charters of important cities like Leyden, Delft and Rotterdam and in the charter of "Great Privilege" of 1477 obtained by Flanders, Brabant, Hainault and Holland when the Dutch and the Flemish were subjects of an illustrious and rich Duchy of Burgundy. All matters concerning wars, royal marriages and taxes required the assent of the estates, and high office was reserved for local citizens. The ruling Grand Council was thoroughly representative and administration, including justice, was decentralised and delegated to the provinces. Later, the confederation of the northern provinces in 1579 brought about a form of government quite remarkably advanced for the age. The Dutch republic endured some two hundred years. In constitutional terms, at its foundation, it was leading the continent. What were the main features of this political entity?

First and foremost there was a decentralisation of power, both hierarchically and geographically. Founded as a confederation of independent provinces, it was natural for these to safeguard their autonomy insofar as possible. At the same time, in order to maintain a united fighting front, principally against the Spanish, then the Habsburgs and the French, the leadership was vested in the office of a

Stadtholder, an office filled in practice by successive princes of the House of Orange, the principal representatives of a residual oligarchy. But the authority of the Stadtholder was heavily circumscribed by the States-General, an effective and active parliament of the country as a whole. Next, one cannot over-estimate the influence of the burghers, a fast rising, powerful middle class composed of administrators, professionals, bankers, traders and craftsmen inhabiting the economically all-important cities, giving rise to a mercantile empire, with the Dutch East India company as its pivot, driven by aggressive entrepreneurs and naval excellence. Even more significantly, political room was afforded to outstanding personalities to exercise their talents to the benefit of the communal interest. Names like Oldenbarneveldt, Hugo Grotius, Piet Hein, John de Witt, Antonius Heinsius are legendary in Holland, though scarcely recognised here. Finally, there was a gradual acceptance and toleration of religious pluralism ranging from the Catholic South to the strict Calvinist North.

Sharing of decision-making powers, dependence on individuals rather than on the system, religious freedoms, are the hallmarks of an eccentric political tradition. The lack of an over-riding central authority became, in fact, the republic's greatest single weakness. Recurring crises and episodic minor revolts centred on tensions between the constituent estates and between the Stadtholder and an increasingly politicised middle class.

After the briefest flirtation with the French Revolution and an interlude of Napoleonic rule, the Netherlands, joined by Belgium, made an easy transition to constitutional monarchy in 1814. The brief merger with Belgium, dissolved in 1830, was followed in 1848, not by the kind of revolution that swept most of the continent, but by the drafting of a new constitution that established full parliamentary rule for the Netherlands once and for all. The extension of the electoral base, the introduction of other measures to enhance individual rights and civil liberties, was, as in Britain, a gradual process. The number of electors rose to 300,000 in 1887, then doubled nine years later. Proportional representation to include the whole population had to wait till the end of World War One.

All in all, the Dutch road to modern democracy was not that dissimilar from the one taken on these islands. It was evolutionary, pragmatic, measured and made for travel by ordinary people.

Scandinavia

The histories of Norway, Denmark and Sweden are closely interwoven and they have, of course, a common Viking root. At one time or other each one of them dominated her neighbours for centuries. They shared many monarchs, and two or sometimes all three, were united at various historical moments only for these unions to dissolve later. They were often the best of allies and as often the worst of enemies, fighting each other to a bloody standstill without quite reaching a lasting settlement of Nordic destinies. Although they tend to play down any similarities in national characteristics, the defining features in political evolution, mind-set and culture, are common to all three nations. Given their roaming, warrior ancestry, sea-faring orientation, and set in relatively small numbers in a vast, often unfriendly terrain which developed self-dependence, it would be surprising were it otherwise.

Submission to central authority never came easy for Scandinavians. Leadership in the Viking world had to be won on the battlefield and allegiance was personal rather than dynastic. Hence the hereditary principle was often challenged, kings and royal heirs were fought, appointed, confirmed, deposed, banished or murdered with monotonous frequency. The continent-wide idea of a sacrosanct monarch, reigning by divine right over a subject people, never had quite the same resonance in Scandinavia. Its remoteness and distance from Rome curtailed the centralising influence of the Catholic Church. Despite the establishment of strong bishoprics, like Uppsala, and assiduous building of cathedrals and churches all over the place, elements of the old religion survived right up to a Reformation that removed Rome from the political equation altogether.

Throughout the long period of nation building, which was accompanied by an inevitable strengthening of monarchical authority, the desire for participation in the political process not only survived but found increasingly tangible expression in constitutional legislation and power sharing. In the mid thirteenth century, for example, Birger Jarl, Sweden's greatest mediaeval statesman and legislator abolished serfdom. A hundred years later, King Magnus summoned the first national Riksdag, with the middle classes represented alongside the nobles and clergy, leading to the first coronation oath and the growth of popular liberties. Meanwhile Denmark established her first *parlamentum* in 1250 and the charter of 1282 legalised the assembly's authority, limiting the king's arbitrary power. A century later, a national assembly at Kalenburg concluded with a two-sided, legally binding contract, setting out the King's and the people's rights and duties. Before the end of the 12th-century, Norway already had the institution of *lagmenn* (lawmen) to act as instructors to juries in the administering of justice.

By the 15th-century the Danish Rigsraad possessed, at least in theory, the highest constitutional powers in the land. In 1500, of a total of 80,000 farms, 12,000 were owned by peasants and a further 48,000 leased to them by the crown, the church or the nobles. The following three centuries of Danish history were a struggle involving monarch, aristocrat, burgher and peasant, in various complex alignments, on the home front. Fortunes of this struggle fluctuated: sometimes the king, with the help of the middle class, gained in power at the expense of the nobility, for example after the constitutional revolution in 1660; at other times burghers gained the upper hand and ran the government, as they did until 1730, when the great landowners wrested back most of the power they lost earlier.

In Sweden, Charles IX, once crowned in 1607, aimed at a monarchical-democratic form of government through a Riksdag that was convened with remarkable frequency. The nobility then succeeded in defending their privileges by founding a Riddarhus, a House of Lords, in 1626. For the greater part of the 18th-century a flourishing two-party political system, the Hats and the Caps, something like the Tories and Whigs, were opposing each other in a Riksdag not that dissimilar, in function and influence, to the House of Commons of the same period.

What is most significant in Scandinavian political evolution is the meaningful role played by the Rigsraad and

Riksdag, the respective parliaments of Denmark and Sweden (Norway being united with Denmark until 1800), throughout the convoluted power struggle. Rooted in ancient tribal assemblies, they provided a forum of debate, a focal point, an enduring source of authority in a shifting scene of uncertain royal succession and fast-moving economic and social change. This inherent tendency for broader consultation, for forming and reforming constitutions, created a political climate in which an independent Norway, Denmark and Sweden could gradually develop, from early in the 19th-century, as sovereign parliamentary democracies with their own, distinct traditions. The transition from autocratic rule to all-inclusive forms of government was not particularly peaceful, or smooth or linear. There were reversals, periods of relative chaos, repressions and occasional bloodshed. Nevertheless, there can be no doubt that the historical pattern of democratic evolution, as well as the political culture, of the Scandinavian countries, in common with the Netherlands and Britain, has an underlying eccentric orientation.

3

A Touch of History -
The Concentrics

Man owes his entire existence to the state,
and has his being within it alone
Hegel

France

Whilst British history took its own eccentric course, what
was happening on the other side of the channel? Four years
after the execution of Charles I in England, France moved
in a diametrically opposite direction. The French civil war,
the Fronde, failed utterly to curtail the powers of the king.
Louis XIV not content with all rights over the bodies of his
subjects also claimed jurisdiction, indirectly, over their
souls in his dispute with the pope. The aristocracy, no
longer trusted after the Fronde to play any part in the
governance of the realm, were used as ornaments to
decorate the opulence of Versailles. Dancing attendance on
the Sun King, their lives were consumed by fashion, gossip,
intrigue and the contest for meaningless precedence. The
peasants on the estates of these absentee landlords, viewed

merely as income-producing assets, enjoyed all the rights and privileges of a mediaeval villain. Some restraints on royal absolutism came from the Church, the high courts of appeal and some representative assemblies still meeting in frontier regions. But their leverage was uncoordinated and totally inadequate to move the country towards gradual reform. When this political system finally failed, in 1789, the States-General, the only institution in France that could claim to represent the nation as a whole, met for the first time since 1614. The French people had simply not been consulted for some 165 years.

Revolutions are not created out of nothing. They also seldom bring a stable democratic government in their wake. The French one set the pattern, giving birth to the Terror and then to the first "modern" dictator who also, incidentally, unified Europe, at least for a brief spell. The French Revolution is as redolent of France as the House of Commons is of Britain. Its worldwide influence is also comparable to that of Westminster, the "mother of parliaments". After all, it inspired the continental convulsions of 1848, the creation of the Soviet Union and Mao's Republic of China, not to mention popular risings in Cuba, Iran and many South American and Middle Eastern countries.

"*Liberté, Egalité, Fraternité*" are emotively rich, noble ideals. In late 18th-century France they represented exactly what the people so grievously lacked. Out of context, they are general, abstract, ill-defined words, more useful in arousing passions than in achieving practical improvements in people's daily life. English equivalents, typically, were more modest, specific and attainable. Freedom meant the attainment of tangible civil liberties, equality referred to equality before the law and brotherhood has been confined to religious associations and trade unions.

Napoleon is, of course, one of the keys to understanding modern French society. He was much more than a military genius who carried French arms to unprecedented triumphs and implanted *La Gloire* in the national psyche, so lovingly and frequently recalled by de Gaulle in our own time. The famous code that he created, that bears his name, forms the basis of the current French legal system and is the enduring model of a state education system and administration that nurtures an elite class designed to govern French social and political life. This self-perpetuating elite, this eminently successful meritocracy, adapted itself to the empires, monarchies, republics and constitutions that have followed each other with regular frequency throughout the last two centuries of French history.

Napoleon's departure restored the Bourbon dynasty in 1815 on a throne loosely constrained by a functioning parliament. This parliament, a shadow of its British counterpart, did not last long. Ultra royalist pressure brought on the Revolution of 1830, placing Louis Philippe, the citizen king, at the head of a more-or-less bourgeois establishment. The beginnings of a parliamentary democracy were nipped in the bud by the revolution of 1848 that signalled the birth of the Second Republic. With a new, almost socialist, constitution that increased the electorate from 200,000 to 9 million in one fell swoop, the country swung from one extreme to the other. This did not matter much since the French grew quickly tired of democracy and within four years Napoleon III was allowed to establish the Second Empire with yet another constitution, approved by yet one more plebiscite, in 1852.

The Second Empire died in the defeat by Prussia some twenty years later, making way for the Third Republic which managed to survive until the country's occupation by Germany in World War Two. To a student of French history its 90-year span presents a bewildering spectacle. The republic's convoluted, and frequently changing, constitutional laws, the complex division of power between the president and the various ministries, between the ministries and the assembly, the fragmentation of parties within the assembly and the feebleness of leaders who could command neither a parliamentary majority nor even the allegiance of their own party, made France virtually ungovernable. In its first two decades, the Third Republic had no fewer than twenty governments. In the five years preceding World War One 10 governments came and went and the critical years of 1929-1936 saw twenty ministerial crises. Aristide Briand, a fervent believer in internationalism, held the post of premier in 11 separate administrations, surely some sort of world record in the annals of democratic bankruptcies. None of these dry statistics truly describes a society in a state of permanent political turmoil, littered with strikes and other forms of direct action, unable to achieve any social cohesion, prey to the unyielding factional interests of workers, clerics, landlords, the military, and ideologues in finely differentiated shades from a Marxist Left to a Monarchist Right.

The comprehensive defeat of France in 1940 brought about the Fourth Republic, that, in political terms, inherited all the ills of the previous one. In 1946-7 Leon Blum's single-party ministry lasted all of six weeks and was followed, in the next five years, by ten different coalitions made up not just by various combinations of several parties but many groupings within each one of them. All in all there were 23 governments in the Republic's twelve-year lifespan. In 1958 the threat of civil war from disaffected generals in Algeria allied to embittered colons (settlers) allowed Charles de Gaulle to assume the Presidency on his own terms. He was granted unlimited powers and a mandate to draft yet another new constitution which inaugurated, after the umpteenth popular referendum, the Fifth Republic. Thus, after ninety years of struggle with a sovereign parliament, the French reverted to a presidential form of government, with decisive powers in the hands of a single individual.

This political framework has been working better than any previous ones tried out in France but it relies on an individual of sufficient stature to secure and maintain the support of the population via a much weakened parliament. This was, in fact, the case from de Gaulle down to Mitterrand. Unfortunately, the tarnished personality of Jacques Chirac, a left-leaning Parliament in opposition and the nasty surprise of an extremist Le Pen, raise disturbing doubts about the ultimate viability of the new model. Another autocratic presidency with a flawed president, as is the case now, and voter apathy may well force a rewriting of the script once more.

The downside of a centrist system is manifest when the centre itself is weak. When a rift between government and the governed breeds grievances, direct action follows. Such has been the pattern of French political life over the last two centuries. Marches and protests are daily events all over the world, but it is the ease with which truckers, farmers, air traffic controllers, railwaymen and just about any small minority group regularly paralyse the country and hold her leaders to ransom, that is so characteristic of politics in France.

In short, throughout the 17th and 18th centuries France was subject to a highly centralised, autocratic form of government. Under this type of regime, she extended her boundaries to those of more or less the present day and established herself as a most influential and pre-eminent European power. Over the course of the next two centuries the French had two empires, two monarchies and five republics. Each transition from one form of government to the next was abrupt, sudden and accompanied by revolution, violence or the threat of force. It is hardly surprising that throughout this period the country exhibited all the ills associated with endemically weak government. After Napoleon, France declined, her influence and power diminished, her military glories waned. She could only save her status and retain her territorial integrity by an intricate web of alliances that contributed in no small measure to two world wars.

Indeed the one field of political activity where France has consistently excelled is foreign affairs. Here she has proved more than a match for her adversaries as well as her allies. Cardinal Richelieu, a prime minister whose true greatness lay in the art of diplomacy, created a legendary prototype to which French ministers have aspired ever since. His masterly performance, emulated by his pupil, Cardinal Mazarin, ensured that France was the only power that benefited materially from the horrors of the Thirty Years War. The 1648 Treaty of Westphalia, regarded for 200 years as the charter for Europe, attached Alsace to France and fatally fragmented Germany with consequences still felt today. The Earl of Bute and the Duke of Bedford were putty in the hands of Duc de Choiseul, a proven master of negotiations, so that the decisive British victories in the Seven Years War yielded less decisive results following the Peace Treaty signed in Paris 1763. Talleyrand returned from the Peace Congress of Vienna in 1816 with France reconfirmed as a Great Power, despite the final and comprehensive loss of the Napoleonic wars.

The British and the Americans saved France in World War One, but the treaty of Versailles in 1919 reflected more the ideas of an experienced "tiger" Clemenceau, than a naive and idealistic Woodrow Wilson, or Lloyd George focused on the British Empire and a philosophically inclined Balfour. After being occupied for much of World War Two, having contributed minimally to the victory of the Allies, France re-emerged miraculously as one of the four major powers with equal shares in settling the fate of Germany. She was even gifted one of the seven permanent seats on the Security Council of the UN, enabling her to use a veto against her benefactors on occasions like the Iraq war. Refusing to participate in the command structure of NATO, the principal instrument of defence against a very real Soviet threat to Europe, France succeeded in excluding Britain from the Common Market long enough to set a new European agenda, seize the leadership of the continent and create a political union in her own Gallic image. An incredible sequence of massive diplomatic achievements.

The two dominant figures in post war-France, de Gaulle and Mitterrand, embody two different aspects of the French political persona: de Gaulle, haughty, obdurate, visionary, idealistic; Mitterrand, shrewd, manipulative, unscrupulous, corrupt; both highly effective and totally committed to the idea of a Greater Europe led by France. It is certainly not a coincidence that the body entrusted with the creation of a pan-European constitution was presided over by the French in the person of Giscard d'Estaing, a convinced integrationist. Those pro-Euro British politicians who blithely envisage sidelining French influence in shaping the future of the EU, must live in cloud cuckoo land, blind to the lessons of history.

The French political culture of today naturally reflects the nation's history. It is inspired by abstract, intellectual ideals for the supposed benefit of a continent whilst in reality being devoted to the fierce defence of national, party and sectional interests. It tends to generate complex, carefully crafted constitutional and administrative documents that have limited practical value. It recognises the need for centralisation but finds any encroachment on personal liberty irritating. It thrives on logic rather than common sense. Its tendency to formalise generates bureaucracy on the grand scale. The proliferation and fragmentation of political movements tends to develop skills in negotiation, manipulation and political manoeuvring, rather than effective, tolerable government.

The point is not that France's attempts at a Westminster-style democracy, so rich in ideals, oratory and literature, have all failed. What matters is the underlying historical tendency to invest political power in a central authority that plans, legislates, administers and implements the nation's business. France is in her element in an essentially concentric political setting where power is held by the few and radiates outward from a strong centre. In major crises, the people in power may be swept aside, the structure may alter but the centre remains firmly in place, dominant as ever.

France's national rail services, often held up as a model to inspire her European neighbours, illustrate the point. Certainly, major rail networks for TGV trains were completed within 3 or 4 years of initial conception. But then the government did not need to go through tiresome procedures consulting people whose land, properties and livelihood lay across the route, nor did they have to hold interminable inquiries as to the effect on bird life, badger habitat, flora and fauna, nor even consider fifteen alternative routes suggested by helpful locals whose sole objective was to shift the whole project elsewhere. Work on the London-Dover Eurostar line is far from complete, some eleven years after Westminster approved it. All Paris has to do is to declare a project "to be in the national interest" and, hey presto, construction begins.

It is possible to have an effective concentric form of government, where the state takes precedence over individuals. It is also possible to have an eccentric form of government, where the interest of each person, each local community, is taken seriously, where every point of view is considered, even if a national issue is at stake. What is not possible is to have the best of both worlds. They happen to be irreconcilable. One suits the French temper, the other has become, for better or worse, the relatively inefficient yet people-friendly way of political life in Britain.

Germany

In November 1518 the Emperor Maximilian rode into Innsbruck. The innkeepers of the town refused to lodge his entourage since moneys were owing to them from a previous visit. To make matters worse, the town council refused an official reception. Maximilian departed in a fury to die elsewhere a few weeks later. This episode suggests that Germanic people, at least in the 16th-century, had quite an impressive degree of local autonomy and were not overawed by their rulers. Indeed, imperial free cities, like Augsburg and Nurnberg, enjoyed rights, privileges and a form of self-government to be found only in the city-states of Italy of earlier periods.

Within each of the free cities, electorates, duchies, bishoprics and the statelets that made up the intricate mosaic of the German-speaking peoples, there was however, no noticeable concerted movement to relax the strict rules and regulations by means of which Teutonic central authorities exercised their control over the lives of the governed. The Peace of Augsburg that ended the German wars of religion in 1555 had ensured that *Kleinstaaterie* ("petty-statery") would prevail with the religion of each ruler determining the religion of the ruled. If anything, the ravages of the Thirty Years War, and the treaty of Westphalia at its conclusion in 1648, sank the political landscape even deeper into a time-warp that lasted until the awakening of a German national consciousness towards the end of the 18th-century.

To appreciate the full force of the drive towards the unification of the German-speaking people that dominated German politics from the 19th-century onward, one has to picture a country so fragmented that it could hardly be considered as a country at all. Primogeniture not being an established principle, princes divided their lands between their sons, thus creating dozens of small independent states within their province, some of them no more than a village with a royal hunting lodge which served as the capital.

Scattered among these princely lands were the bishoprics linked to Rome as well as free cities of vastly varying possessions, some owning whole provinces, while others just tidy orchards about their walls. There were even free imperial villages. Innumerable free knights and counts owed allegiance only to the Emperor himself. Thus a population of twenty-one million depended for its government on more than two thousand separate authorities. No mechanism of imperial government could possibly control such an agglomeration of diverse and often conflicting entities.

As a cohesive nation state Germany was some three hundred years behind Spain, France and England. This fact goes some way, perhaps, to explain why liberal and democratic ideas, so rife in the rest of 19th-century Europe, received such short shrift in nascent Germany. The Germans were just too busy becoming a nation to worry about individual rights and liberties. A promise given to the Prussian people in 1815 to establish a representative assembly took over thirty years to fulfil and after its first meetings, this diet was irretrievably dissolved. Similarly, the revolutions of 1848 in Prussia, Austria and most of the other states within the German ambit, resulted in even less liberal and delegated forms of government than the ones before the upheavals.

The Prussian administration of 1859, hailed as inaugurating a new liberal rule, stumbled three years later on the issue of a military budget expanded without parliamentary authorisation. It was at this point that the spectacular career of Otto von Bismarck took off. He managed to govern Prussia and Germany for the next 26 years without much regard for the various elected diets, assemblies and parliaments. Perhaps the decisive moment in modern German history was the passing of an act by 230 votes to 75 in the Prussian parliament in 1866 to indemnify Bismarck's unconstitutional collection of taxes. The money was needed to fight the decisive war with Austria which gave Prussia the leadership of the German people. The approval of this act meant that the Prussian liberals, until then genuine opponents of Bismarck, dropped their insistence on parliamentary sovereignty in exchange for the prospect of German unity. Thus Germany was never destined to become a constitutional monarchy. Although Germans were given, at a stroke, universal suffrage, press freedom, uniform legal procedure and municipal autonomy in the 1870s, when it came to deciding between war and peace in 1914, it was the Emperor and the Prussian military establishment, and not the Reichstag, who had the final say.

The interwar period demonstrated once more, if any demonstration was needed, that when it came to a choice between a strong central authoritarian leadership and a truly democratic government, Germany would always submit herself willingly to the former. The Weimar Republic (1918-1933), an attempt at parliamentary democracy, never had the full support of the German people, and was disdained by the German army.

The current Federal German constitution, and her parliamentary democracy, is not a German creation, is not rooted in German political culture and is alien to her political traditions. It was drafted by Germans in occupied Germany, under heavy British and American guidance and supervision. The federal structure is modelled on Anglo-Saxon democratic principles with the aim of giving the

Lander (provinces) greater autonomy and so preventing centralisation of power. But no matter how carefully any German constitution is crafted or how strictly parliamentary elections are conducted, democracy sits uneasily on German shoulders. The German people are essentially leader led. Bismarck, William II, Hitler, Konrad Adenauer, Willy Brandt, Helmut Kohl had at least this much in common: they exercised effective power for considerable periods of time, they became figures of authority, they gained the personal following and the trust of the people, they were autocratic rulers in fact, in style, even if not always in name. The fate of the powerful and respected Deutschemark, the single most important icon of Germany's post-war success, was sealed by the Maastricht Treaty. Yet the people of Germany were not consulted before the treaty was agreed nor were they asked to endorse it afterwards. Not even Mitterrand in concentric France dared to ignore his nation to such an extent.

Hitler is generally considered a historical aberration. The magnitude of the devastation he caused, the enormity of his crimes, certainly make him unique. But in terms of inspiring a whole nation, in gaining the love and obedience of the people, in his mastery over them, he is very much part of the German political tradition. The fact that the Hitler phenomenon occurred in Germany is no accident. No one claims that the Germans, as individuals, are less moral than members of any other race. Nor do they lack a sense of communal responsibility. What makes German political life distinctive is the degree of subservience of individuals to abstract concepts and the authority of the state. This authority tends to be vested in the figure of a leader, a leader respected, followed and obeyed. Rules are generated from the centre and, on the whole, people are comfortable in conforming.

The dominance of the centre, the acceptance of *raison d'état* as an over-riding imperative, the conforming individual and the drive from top down, are the essential characteristics of a concentric society. There is no danger of another Hitler in the foreseeable future, his effect on the nation has been too cathartic for that. But nor is there an immediate prospect of a profound change in the inbred German political instinct, an instinct diametrically opposed to the British one.

Spain

After Ferdinand and Isabella, the Catholic monarchs, purged a unified Spain of Jews and Moors, it was left to Philip II, three generations later, to set the pattern of government for the next three centuries. Through a rigidly observed system of councils and committees, all decisions were taken by the King personally. There was no delegation of authority. As communication was mainly in writing, Philip would read, annotate and approve several hundred documents daily. As he abhorred the Reformation in all its guises, enormous pressure was exercised on any individual who might deviate in the slightest from the Catholic norm. Whether ecclesiastic or secular, central authority was absolute. Non-conformity was simply not tolerated. The power of the Cortes of Aragon, Valencia and Catalonia were heavily curtailed whilst those of the Inquisition were strengthened. The stage was set for the most profound and longest lasting concentric political tradition on the continent.

Philip's successors followed suit and when the Bourbons

replaced the Habsburgs in 1700, the absolutist and centralising tendencies developed even further. Thus, by the end of 18th century the single remaining Cortes, the sole representative body of the nation, was reduced to little more than a rubber stamp. The 19th-century was punctuated by successive Carlist wars, revolutions, brief attempts at establishing republican rule, army interventions to restore authority and order and intermittent episodes of constitutional government with some parliamentary input.

Spain was spared the horrors of the First World War, but in its aftermath the country became virtually ungovernable. The collapse of the seven-year dictatorship of Primo de Rivera signalled the end of the Monarchy. The Second Republic, Spain's brief flirtation with full-scale democracy, resulted in one of most vicious civil wars ever fought. Although the recent transition from Franco's dictatorship to constitutional monarchy has gone surprisingly smoothly, the country's democratic grassroots are still young, tender and vulnerable. Concentric traditions, so deeply ingrained, of such long duration, do not change in one, two or three generations.

4

A Touch of History:
The Italian Exception

Governing Italy is not difficult, it is merely futile
Mussolini

The political history of the people living in the Italian peninsula is perhaps the most fascinating, bewildering and instructive of them all. There is no governmental system that has not had its day in one or other part of this land. Indeed, many of them were invented, developed and refined here. As early as the 13th-century, democratically inspired communes created administrative structures of remarkable political sophistication with statutes, councils and executive branches of their own. The first genuine adversarial political parties on the continent, Guelph and Ghibeline, fought their battles across state lines well into the 14th-century.

In common with the rest of mediaeval Europe, Italy was not short of *parliamenti*, assemblies of estates with an amazing array of complex privileges and rights as between king, church, aristocracy and citizens of towns. Where Italy differed from other continental states was its sharp territorial division into three distinct regions. The kingdoms of Sicily and Naples in the South retained a traditional, absolutist form of monarchic government until nearly the 19th-century. Her foreign rulers had little knowledge of, and even less concern for, the native population. In the centre, at the heart of Italy, the papal states centred on Rome, enjoyed a virtually uninterrupted theocratic government considerably more rigorous than that of the Mullahs in present day Iran. Whilst the extent of territories under direct Vatican control fluctuated over thirteen centuries, papal intervention, political, financial and military, had a profound effect throughout the peninsula. It was in the north, however, that the vibrant political life of expanding city states created many of the more interesting forms of government. Towns like Padua, Pisa, Genoa, Siena, Ferrara, Bologna, Florence and, of course, Venice, originally evolved as republics with a high degree of democratic content. Craftsmen, merchants and professionals, whose skill and industry generated the communities' prosperity, were basically in charge. Citizens of these republics were being regularly consulted, there was an open forum for debate and people in general were free to run their own affairs.

As the towns grew in wealth and ambition, as they started to absorb greater and greater chunks of surrounding countryside, owners of estates and feudal traditions had to be accommodated within the republican format. The increase in size and conflicting political outlook made governing more difficult and, as is often the case, it also resulted in the erosion of democracy. So we see emerging a consular office, the appointment of a single executive magistrate, a podesta, and the rise of Signorie, governments controlled by signori elected by councils for life with more or less unlimited powers. Originally the signori owed their authority to a measure of communal consent and so at least the republican framework, if not its spirit, were preserved. Once succession became hereditary however, it was easy to establish ducal dynasties, replacing the vestiges of democracy with centralised, autocratic rule. The Visconti in Milan, the Este in Ferrara, the Carrarra in Padua and the Gonzaga in Mantua, were all well ensconced by the middle of the 14th-century. Florence, Bologna and some other towns bucked the trend, at least for a while. Florence even managed to expel the Medicis twice before the republic was forced to yield and centuries of democratic tradition were sacrificed for Florence to become part of a unified Tuscan dukedom.

As the great exception to the continuous political turmoil, social upheaval, fragile government or despotic rule within the states that formed so fragmented a peninsula, the serene republic of Venice kept its eccentric independence for one thousand years. Throughout, a highly effective form of government retained limited, but significant, democratic content. Severe limitations imposed on the power of the Doge from the 11th-century onwards removed the possibility of dynastic rule. Even when the restricted composition of the great council three hundred years later turned Venice into a classic oligarchy, clearly defined lines of authority between the senate, the council of ten, the cabinet and the Doge himself, provided enough checks and balances against potential misappropriation and abuse of power. Elections to these bodies were conducted by a highly complex system of secret ballot and tenure of office was strictly short-term, sometimes less than a year. Only the Doge was chosen for life but, as the average age at election was over seventy, incumbents never lasted long enough to create a permanent power base. Entry into the ranks of the few hundred families who controlled the levers of power was never easy. On the other hand, even if his family's name was not inscribed in the famed Libro d'Oro, an ordinary citizen was freer, better protected, had greater opportunities and privileges than the minor nobility in most, if not all, contemporary European states. For example, the office of Grand Chancellor, the effective head of the Republic's entire civil service, was explicitly reserved for the cittadini. Elected for life, he ranked above Senators, and was entitled to a funeral of similar proportions to that of the Doge himself.

That Venice should have valued its citizens so highly is hardly surprising. Founded on a small, barren lagoon, with virtually no natural resources, all she ever had was the industry, skill, enterprise, talent and courage of her people. Venice succeeded in harnessing this rich human resource, building the city into the centre of a mercantile empire without compare. Her genius lay in developing an original form of centralised government without inhibiting the inventiveness and initiative of the individual. Elizabethan England came perhaps closest to the Venetian model, but as a historical lesson to other countries, in other ages, Venice never played a significant role.

By the 18th-century the empire was in terminal decline. Global trade routes having fatally shifted, her traders, once bestriding the Mediterranean, were virtually confined to the Republic's shrinking boundaries. As a financial centre she was a shadow of her former dominant self. The navy, the backbone of the empire, that helped wipe out the entire Turkish fleet in the famous battle of Lapento in 1571, was dead. The Arsenale shipyard, that at its zenith produced the best naval vessels in the world at the rate of one per day, was now lying idle. It was left to her theatres, spectacular pageants, grand palaces, singing gondoliers and luxurious lifestyle to continue dazzling the world.

After centuries of endless warring, the rest of the peninsula had become by then a backwater of a fast developing western world, most of it in the possession of the Spanish Bourbon and Austrian royal houses. The few political reforms accomplished were made in the interests of the despot, imposed without consulting the people and carried out mostly by alien rulers. The long process of uniting the peninsula into a single cohesive political entity began sometime in the 19th-century, after the collapse of the Napoleonic system. It is still ongoing and may well be interminable. For although Italy has fixed geographic boundaries, a flag, a national anthem, an army, a police force, an excellent football team and many other attributes associated with a sovereign state, she has failed to establish a viable form of government acceptable to the people and enforceable throughout the country. It is not for lack of trying. Over the last 150 years or so she has experimented with constitutional monarchy, democracies of various sorts, fascism, a myriad of political parties, different electoral systems, regional autonomies and even organised chaos. All in vain.

The jigsaw of political Italy has long been divided along several intersecting lines: rural and urban, Catholics and secularists, peasants and landlords, working classes and industrialists, middle classes and aristocracy, the regions and Rome, North and South, etc. Whilst some such divisions did play a part in the politics of other European states at one time or other, they have been peculiarly persistent in Italy, making for a complexity that has proved impossible to accommodate effectively within the framework of a parliamentary democracy, or indeed any other form of government. The political cycle took roughly the following pattern: an attempt to govern by clever manipulation of a coalition of interests (e.g. Giolitti, four times premier 1892-1921), breakdown of government, chaos, autocratic rule under a strong leader (e.g. Crispi, Mussolini), revolt and back to *transformismo*.

In matters of political experimentation, the Italians have been richly inventive. For long periods of the 19th-century bitter personal animosities and near anarchical individualism made regular party political life in parliament impossible, so *transformismo* came into being as the only means of keeping governments going. Under this system, irrespective of election results, a large amorphous centre coalition could stay in power indefinitely by a slight shift of policy and by rotating the principal personalities with every crisis. This idea has the short-term advantage of appearing to respond to real issues whilst doing little in reality. It has the long-term drawback of practically disenfranchising the electorate. *Transformismo* not only became respectable in Italy but was even exported to France where it was further refined and proved to be hugely popular in the first half of the last century. Similarly, Fascism was an original Italian invention. The later dictatorships of Stalin, Hitler and Franco were tainted by consistent ideologies, Marxist, Nazi or Falangist, whereas that of Mussolini was purely personal. Fascism was whatever, at any given moment, the Duce decided it had to be. It was as arbitrary as that.

With a slim, elongated body, a head in the snowy peaks of central Europe and feet dangling in the sultry Mediterranean, the governing of Italy can never be simple. She cannot even qualify as an extreme example of an eccentric state, for such a state must still have an effective executive centre of power sustained by grass-root support. This does not mean that Italian people lack political traditions or that they are worse off than their European neighbours. On the contrary, life prospers and a strong sense of humanity, tolerance and freedom prevails everywhere. This is because, first, the rulers and the ruled have a polite disregard for each other, and second, the primary allegiance of the people is to the family and not the state. The meaning of "family" in Italy goes well beyond the nuclear unit; it encompasses the extended clan, the local community, club, co-workers and any close-knit organisation that the individual belongs to. The impact of laws, directives, rules or regulations emanating from a remote centre pales in comparison with the imperatives on the doorstep. Italy's failure to become an effective political entity is compensated by the strength and vitality of her local communities. In Britain, social cohesion is achieved by the rule of law and individual responsibility. In Italy it is secured by family links and a powerful sense of community.

5

Authority and The Individual

*Whereas in England all is permitted that is not expressly
prohibited, it has been said that in Germany all is
prohibited unless expressly permitted and
in France all is permitted that
is expressly prohibited*
Robert Megarry

Are the differences in government cultures between
eccentric and concentric nations the result of historic
accident? Are they superficial, transitory, confined to
politics? Or are they more deeply rooted in the national
mindset with corresponding traits manifest outside
politics? Two subjects, not unrelated to each other, may
provide a clue: response to authority and respect for the
individual.

Germans instinctively obey their formal superiors, be
they Chancellors, bank officials, department heads or
parking attendants. They appreciate transparent
hierarchies, uniforms and unambiguous rules. Those in
authority, those who wear the uniform, exercise power by
issuing explicit orders that are seldom questioned, almost

never challenged. It is simply assumed that whoever gives them has the right to do so. Figures of authority may dominate even without uniform or title. The critic Reich Ranicki has become the arbiter of German post-war literature single-handed. His word is sufficient to sell novels in hundreds of thousands or kill others stone dead. Similarly, the annual official "Game of the Year" accolade ensures that some half-a-million families must have the winning game. Powerful critics and critical awards abound in all other cultures but their tangible influence comes nowhere near the German scale.

Such attitudes, of course, confer a huge advantage on industry and administration. Conformity, order, clearly delineated duties, legible marks of status, adherence to rules, are the basics of good organisation. It is the native instinct for organisation, wedded to an all-pervasive work ethic that makes for German efficiency and provides the foundation of her economic superiority. This native talent for organisation is an acknowledged feature of German sport, particularly team sport, in the international arena. Their soccer teams won two world cups, as well as two European cups and have been a permanent fixture in the final stages of virtually all major competitions, without truly great stars like Pele, Cruyf, Di Stefano, George Best, Puskas, Ronaldo, etc. They even beat the legendary, unbeaten Hungarian side in the 1954 final in Zurich by sheer organisation alone.

As for the reverse side of the coin, respect for the individual is not generally associated with the German mentality. This is not to say that individual contributions to a community, a business, a team or a project are not appreciated. On the contrary, it is precisely in terms of such contribution to the greater whole that the individual is perceived and valued. Once an individual ceases to be useful, that is more or less the end of him. He may be kind, or amusing, or wise, or cheerful, but his individuality does not matter, it does not count. The sick, the pensioners, the unemployed are probably better cared for in Germany than elsewhere in Europe, it is just the respect of their fellow creatures that is missing.

British attitudes stand in stark contrast to all this. People hereabouts are not exactly impressed by authority. They are asked to do things, not given orders. When faced with government or business directives, they tend to ask questions, express doubts and mostly comply only if they find it makes sense. "Please refrain from…" is more prevalent than "It is forbidden to…" Managers do not automatically command the respect of the managed, they have to earn it. Pulling rank tends to be counterproductive. Rules and regulations are considered irksome and, unless unavoidable, are often ignored. Typically, those who are supposed to lead, especially if they are even slightly pompous, become figures of fun and are savaged by a sense of humour far more deadly to authority than any insubordination or revolt. Hitler, with his screeching hyperbole, goose-stepping and salutes, would never have made it past the soapboxes of Hyde Park Corner; Sir Oswald Mosley just managed it to jail. Nobody on the continent will ever understand how Churchill, with the nation's deserved gratitude ringing in his ears, at the height of his power, in the moment of his greatest triumph, could have been unceremoniously bundled out of office. It could never have happened anywhere else.

British resistance to anything smacking of a cult of

personality is part of daily life. Stars in the world of entertainment, sport, business, all those achievers of note who are brought to public prominence, are considered fair game for a ravenous press. Minor imperfections in their private or professional lives are eagerly seized on to diminish stature and tarnish success. This pursuit does not merely apply to the living. Biographers seem to have been engaged over the last fifty years in a campaign to deconstruct most of the well-loved icons of the past. British political, literary, scientific, military and industrial history appear to have been peopled by pigmies or giants with feet of clay.

There is a perception abroad, as well as at home, that Britain is particularly class conscious. Love of ceremony, history and tradition should not be confused with a rigid caste system. Certainly inter-marriage and mobility between social classes has been, if anything, easier here than on the continent. The proverbial doffing of the cap must have been carried out in the past, one suspects, with a bit of an inward smirk and a lot of tongue in cheek. One is hard put to find a Disraeli in mid 19th-century Europe, or a miner's grandson (Harold Macmillan) and a grocer's daughter (Margaret Thatcher), as *conservative* prime ministers on the continent a hundred years later on.

Such an attitude to authority has consequences. Industry, commerce, the service sector, the NHS, transport and society in general, pay a heavy price. The British are perceived, with much justification, as hopelessly inefficient and pretty careless. The rail disasters, the hospital bungles make news because they are deadly and spectacular. The same human failings are rife in every sphere of daily life. If a bank transaction is correct, if a delivery is made on time, if a repair job goes according to plan, it is a surprise. People expect the waitress not to know what is the soup of the day, as they expect the service engineer to ask whether they happen to have a screwdriver when he appears with a cheerful "What's the trouble then, Mate?" on the doorstep.

Every national disaster brings in its wake clamours for a thorough government inquiry. After years of labour, an august body brings forth recommendations of specific technical reforms and new detailed procedures. No published inquiry focuses on individual negligence, no one person is ever held totally responsible, culprits very seldom are brought to court. Trains will shortly be prevented from going through red lights by an infallible gimmick, since the drivers are far too busy to spot them. Besides, they cannot be expected to do their job for 100 per cent of the time. But any system, any prescribed procedure is only as good as the human beings working it. The truth of the matter is that the British are innately casual, easy going, unsystematic and careless. Over the last four or five generations educational institutions have focused on emotional well being, self-expression, creative freedom, exploration and discovery at the expense of routine, accuracy, factual knowledge, discipline and meticulous execution of work and this has merely served to underline a deeply ingrained national trait.

On the other hand, it is difficult for someone born and bred on this island to appreciate fully the consideration accorded to the individual by society here as against elsewhere in the world. This goes well beyond the obvious protection in law vis-à-vis the state, police, employers, salesmen, neighbours and sundry intruders who may or may not disturb the tranquillity of an individual's home. It takes into account the views of every single objector to a new bypass, down to the lowliest form of pond life. In what other country would the construction of a £150 million, six-lane bridge be suspended while a new home was found for a colony of the 8 mm tentacled lagoon worm? It must be reassuring to know that the Environment Agency have put in place a monitoring program to check the well-being of *Alkmaria romijni* in their new home. Despite some racist behaviour, the general level of tolerance displayed towards different incoming ethnic groups is one of the highest in Europe. Benign interest is shown in the maverick, the original, the non-conformist who, more often than not, is a troublemaker and a nuisance to everyone around. Such individuals, if not actually encouraged, are accepted within the community with remarkable ease.

It is natural for people to do their own thing. Pigeon racing, train spotting, rowing across the Atlantic, growing giant marrows, bird watching, fishing, walking the hills, breeding corgis are very British activities. They are also often solitary. People all over the world enjoy their gardens, but nowhere else has gardening become an occupation, and gardens an object of abiding devotion for many millions. The great majority of people own their own homes and do much of the work on them rather than employing experts who, unlike those on the continent, are not held in high regard. Enterprise, initiative and self-dependence are the qualities associated with what is best in the British tradition. They have been instrumental in building a reasonably successful empire. They are all virtues centred on the individual, nurtured over centuries, engrained in British culture. Governors of distant, isolated outposts, were expected to make their own assessment, use their own judgement. Merchant adventurers used their own capital, and took their own risks, in enterprises that eventually gained Britain most of her overseas possessions. Maybe such a history helped to foster British attitudes or maybe these very attitudes created the history. What matters in the end is a national trait of vesting ultimate authority in the individual rather than in the state. In no other country could a prime minister say, as Margaret Thatcher did, no matter how controversially, that there is no such thing as society.

The focus on the individual does not, of course, prevent Britain from organising herself into a cohesive force. But she is better at it in the face of imminent danger, or in the midst of a national emergency, and then mostly at the last minute, with great improvisation. Steve Redgrave, Daley Thompson and the English Rugby team, are recent, untypical, heroes. The British stereotype is a weekend pilot who climbs into an ill prepared fighter with insufficient fuel on board and then proceeds to shoot down three enemy planes before ditching into the sea and swimming ashore for a couple of pints with the boys.

The French response to authority is, as may be expected, more complex. Perhaps the best word to describe it is *mefiance*. Faced with a new directive, rule or instruction coming from above, any self-respecting Frenchman will feel suspicious and resentful. His immediate instinct is one of defiance that will translate itself into protest, or some sort of direct non-compliant action, or an indirect, evasive personal act of damage limitation. To suspect the content of any written document is second nature to the French – history has taught them never to take anything at face value. Resentment at any manifestation of authority derives from deeply held beliefs that all authority is ultimately arbitrary and logically unjustified. Protests of all kinds, the blocking of roads or ports by farmers or truck drivers, strikes by postmen or teachers or air traffic controllers are part of daily life in France – an ongoing, inevitable reality. Nobody is too concerned about it, the alternative being major civil disorder, chaos or revolution.

French tax authorities assume, quite rightly, that tax payers will do their level best not to pay tax. They are less sophisticated and inventive than the British in producing tax avoidance schemes, but they more than make up for it in the size of their black economy, the notorious hoarding and smuggling of money, manipulation and under-declaration of income. At the same time, ordinary people have every reason to suspect authority since it has been the country's age-long custom for those in charge to entrench and widen their power, using it for personal benefit. It has been openly acknowledged in France that the current President is corrupt. Now, after his double election victory, Chirac has set about wielding his power with a vengeance. He imposed his own men in the posts of parliamentary speaker, police chief and head of the Pompidou Centre, in addition to replacing half the prefects, the effective governors of France's provinces. The President now controls the Parliament, the Senate, the Constitutional Council, local government and an array of other bodies including the state broadcasting authority. Not bad for a leader of a European democracy who, on the first ballot, managed to secure the support of less than a fifth of his compatriots.

Charles Bremner, the Paris correspondent of *The Times*, in a recent article, hits the nail on the head when he describes the manner in which France views power and those who hold it. He says "That there is still...a reverence for the *dignity* and prestige of public office...but not in Britain, with its fierce media and knock-about view of politics. The respect flows from the presidency to prime minister and all the way down to *Monsieur le Maire*...this deference still spares the governing classes from the full gaze of *la France d'en bas*, the *down below French* as Prime Minister Raffarin calls the voters."

When it comes to respect for the individual, Frenchmen are deeply conscious of their dignity, aware of the respect they are intrinsically owed. They are proud of their possessions, strongly attached to their property and assertive of any rights they believe they have. This powerful sense of personal entitlement does not make for easy neighbours but it does ultimately protect the individual from encroachment by others on his or her private life. Although not given to eccentricity, the French are highly particular in whatever they do. Nothing is thoughtless, everything matters. They also feel they ought to be free to do what they bloody well like. The combination of these factors makes concerted *positive* action, at all levels, exceeding difficult. Membership does not come easily to the French. The kind of village, club or professional ad hoc committee life, so natural to the English, is a real struggle in France. Self-help networks largely extinguished in the Revolution have never been subsequently revived. Perhaps it is this very French kind of individuality that demands concentric government, to maintain a viable nation state.

Relations between central authorities and individuals in Italy are simpler than that. If you have occasion to travel on trains anywhere on the peninsula, you will notice that some compartments have prominent red no-smoking notices affixed to their windows and doors. You are also likely to observe most of the passengers in these compartments puffing merrily away, with the conductor sublimely indifferent on his ticket inspection tour. For Italians, the preferred way of dealing with centrally imposed rules and regulations is to ignore them. The favoured response by Italian authorities to non-compliance is to turn a blind eye. As against that, loyalty and respect for family, clan and community assumes the role of the higher authority and is, for the individual, virtually of mafia proportions.

6

Justice, Fairness and the Law

No English institutions are more distinctively English
than the Inns of Court...unchartered, unprivileged,
unendowed, without remembered founders...
we shall hardly find their like elsewhere
F.W. Maitland

Orley Farm is one of Trollope's best and least known works. The romantic lead is taken by an idealistic young lawyer but the true hero of the novel is British justice, portrayed with consummate skill by the most acute of literary observers of 19th-century society. The story of a forged will, set against the background of manipulative barristers, masterful cross examinations of weak witnesses, impressionable juries, ending with the wrong verdict, depicts accurately the distinctive features of the administration of the law in this country. The scene painted is not that dissimilar to the present-day world of Rumpole. Trollope and Mortimer, both politically sophisticated, both highly critical, are only too well aware of weaknesses within the system, of miscarriages of justice, of opinionated judges, of amenable juries, yet one is left with the clear impression that neither author would willingly exchange British justice for its continental counterpart. Probably, because the two sets of laws, the two ways of dispensing justice are many miles apart. Jury trials, Habeas Corpus and the notion that one is innocent until *proved* guilty, form a heritage not lightly given up.

Laws and legal procedures vary from country to country but on the continent they share a source, an approach, a history, a culture almost wholly alien to Britain. The origins of Roman law, as that of most legal procedures, lie in some sort of codification of existing customs that govern the ordered lives of a coherent people. The thousand years between the issue of the Twelve Tables, marking the beginning in 451 BC, and its final achievement in the compilation of Justinian's Code in the sixth century, transformed Rome and, inevitably, Roman law too. From a statelet on the banks of the Tiber, Rome grew into a world empire and from what was a relatively simple clarification and recording of oral custom, Roman law, in the hands of professional lawyers, developed into a complex, highly sophisticated technical instrument not readily accessible to the vast majority of the citizens whose life was ruled by it. It was this powerful instrument that largely shaped the legal life of continental Europe.

Roman law invaded European legal practice very slowly. Throughout the early middle ages, even the simplified remnants of a once classic edifice, the "vulgar law", went mostly beyond the comprehension of the assemblies of freemen who discharged justice, according to custom, within Gothic, Frankish, Saxon and other tribal societies. By the 12th-century Roman law, rediscovered, revitalised and reinterpreted, made its presence increasingly felt. Why?

There were three impelling forces at work: the church, secular powers and academia.

Ecclesiastical courts operated in the Latin language, preferably in its written, rather than oral, form. The architects of Canon law sought to standardise procedure and endow decrees with judicial legitimacy emanating from a higher authority. The ultimate aims of the medieval church were to regulate not only the lives of its own servants but also those of all its adherents. The Roman church and Roman law have always been natural allies. They were made for each other.

The compilers of *Liber extra* and *Liber sextus*, the foundations of Canon law, drew their material from papal decretals, which owed a great deal to Roman law. There were some areas of overlap, and of course rivalry between them as to competence and priority. After all, sin can insinuate itself into just about any type of human activity. The two disciplines were taught side by side at the University of Bologna. The expression *utrumque ius* (each law) applied to students of both subjects and also denoted a connection that became more and more intimate. For a quite a while the practitioners of both laws were often interchangeable. Some lawyers were clerics and many clerics pleaded in secular courts.

"What has pleased the prince has the force of law." Justinian's Code, and the later Digest, both part of the *Corpus Juris Civilis*, categorically assert the emperor's absolute power to legislate. It is hardly surprising therefore that rulers, intent on legitimising their own status and keen to assert unbridled authority, should turn to Roman law, encourage its study and propagate its practice. From the German Frederick Barbarossa to Frederick II in Sicily, to

Ferdinand III in Spain, to the Kings of France and Dukes of Burgundy, the pattern repeats itself.

The pervasive influence of Roman law owed as much to the continental academic establishment as to the church and secular ruling princes. The Universities of Bologna in Italy, Salamanca in Spain, Montpellier, Orleans and Paris in France, Heidelberg and Cologne in Germany and finally Leyden in Holland became successively great centres of jurisprudence. It was in these refined halls of pure intellect that Roman law, once researched and studied, and having absorbed local customary forms of justice, was eventually synthesised into the law of the land. It was here that lawyers acquired their technical skills. It was here that expert legal opinion was habitually sought and dispensed *ex cathedra*. By the 16th-century in Germany, in particular, appeals by the courts to the law faculty of the local university were so customary that it was formally included in the imperial criminal law issued by Charles V in 1532.

In the hands of academics the subject of law as a whole, not just its Roman version, slowly and surely developed into a so-called science, the domain of the privileged few. These Doctors of Law claimed, rather arrogantly, the status of *milites legum*, the legal equivalent of military knights. The philosopher Leibnitz even tried to construct a legal universe, derived logically from first truths. He was followed a few years later by the French scholar Jean Domat who tried the same geometric exercise starting from Christian principles. This was a world far removed from the more humble environs of the Inns of Court around Chancery Lane.

Typically, the creation of a national legal system on the continent was not merely a slow, evolutionary process.

From time to time, an irresistible urge impelled European rulers to have produced a custom-made, comprehensive, rational code of law. The *Recopilacion* in Castile in 1567, the work of Jean Baptiste Colbert, the Sun King's Chancellor, the *Codex Teresianus* of 1766 drafted on the orders of Maria Teresa of Austria, the Napoleonic *Code Civil* of 1804, still in force today, are notable instances. Such exercises were usually initiated by "progressive" rulers, often with good intent and always having the unification of their domains well to the fore. Frederick the Great, for example, had as his objective a Prussian code, written in German, comprehensive, clear and certain, to help his people lead a perfect, rational life. Such lofty goals did not prevent him from carting off to prison an entire set of judges from the state's highest appeal court because he was upset by a single verdict. The final text, enacted in 1794, comprises 19,000 articles and deals with everything under the sun, not forgetting intimate relations between husband and wife. It seems to echo the Brussels Bible of 80,000 pages currently in use.

The legal culture of the continent, founded on the written word, driven by the central authorities of church and state intent on control and uniformity, rationalised in the rarefied air of academic establishments, is profoundly concentric in character. The laws, many of them enacted in periods of absolutist rule, tend to be more protective of entrenched society, rather than the individual. Having such strong Latin and academic roots, the administration of justice is highly technical, guided by the letter, not by the spirit of the law. Emphasis is placed more on documentation, less on oral testimony and live cross examination. Sentences are mandatory with hardly any room for individual discretion. Those dispensing justice are functionaries of the state with no separation between the executive and judicial arms of the government. The magistrates in France, the judges in Germany, are specialised professionals, trained civil servants, whose career prospects are dependent on a Ministry of Justice. Neither as solicitors nor as barristers will they have been schooled in the rough and tumble of daily life in the courts. As for the man in the street, the intricacies of procedure, the interminable bureaucracy, the lack of court-room drama, ensure that he is left out of the equation altogether.

It is difficult not to be amazed how different legal life is in Britain. After all, the starting point was not dissimilar. Customary tribal laws both here and on the continent were generated by assemblies. Resolution of cases by oath-gathering and ordeal were common and ecclesiastical courts ruled uniformly throughout Christendom. Indeed, attempts at codification were made in England as early as the 12th-century when Henry II introduced royal courts throughout the land. The *Bracton* compilation of English laws and customs, written in the 1230s, remains the exceptional but vain attempt to render the English Common law in a comprehensive, rational, systematic format. Interestingly, the author of *Bracton*, in anticipation of things to come, places the King under, not above, the law. Although Henry VIII founded Regius Chairs of civil law in Oxford and Cambridge, to replace suppressed chairs of canon law, in stark contrast to the continent, it was not Roman law, not the church, not central government, not Oxbridge that shaped the legal culture of this country.

The law, habits of legislation, court procedure and judiciary bodies in Britain, like parliamentary life, evolved slowly, piecemeal, without any dramatic milestones. English law was not formulated at any given date by a body of technical experts as a coherent set of rules to enhance the well-being of a state. It grew organically out of diverse local tribal customs which, with the merger of tribes into a single people, fused into one set of shared rules: hence the *Common* Law. Such origins are not uncommon, what is remarkable is that it withstood for over ten centuries all the centralising pressures of church, state and university, to retain its integrity and relevance to this very day.

How come? The Reformation, deleting Rome from the equation, may have helped but only to a limited extent. Legal practice in Scotland, where the Reformation took a more radical turn, is more closely associated with that of the continent. The legal life of Germany, grounded on Protestant Prussia, has little in common with what goes on here. The contribution of a powerful parliament, centuries before anything like it emerged on the continent, has certainly been more significant. Apart from maintaining its customary decentralising influence and safeguarding judicial independence, parliament itself acted as a role model of open debate with opposing parties subject to more or less impartial rules. The House could be swayed by argument and oratory just like the jury often is in a court of law. But the answer to the question is more interesting.

The Common Law does not consist of a series of general rules to be applied to specific instances or of a body of abstract principles from which such rules may be derived. It is simply an ever-growing accretion of judgements delivered by individual judges at various times, on a case-by-case basis, over many centuries. The judgements themselves are not aspirational, they are not about how people ought to manage their affairs in an ideal world. They are based on an ongoing reality, on what people may be expected to do in the here and now. The determining question is always about what an ordinary member of the public can reasonably be expected to do in the given circumstances. As the behaviour patterns of the population change, so do the judgements. At one time, it was considered reasonable to restrict aggrieved husbands to the use of a stick no thicker than their little finger when disciplining their wives. Nowadays men may seek relief in the courts from persecution by their aggressive female partners. The point is that judgements seek to reflect prevailing custom, not set new social trends.

Common Law is obviously an academic nightmare. "Turning from the study of the English to the Roman law, you escape from the empire of chaos and darkness to a world which seems by comparison, the region of order and light", this was the observation of John Austin, Professor of Jurisprudence at University College London in the 1830s. But it is, of course, this very quality of *chaos* and *darkness* that gives the Common Law the enduring flexibility, the ability to modify itself and respond to an illogical, none too well organised and fast changing world.

The same chameleon quality, being so ill defined, amorphous, difficult to pin down, goes beyond the Common Law to other aspects of English legal culture. It enables the transforming of laws and legal bodies, so they perform functions altogether removed from those originally intended without recourse to legislative surgery. When Henry II introduced lay juries, they were meant to act, whether grand assizes or indicting juries, as an executive arm of the royal Chancery, part and parcel of the central government being imposed on 12th-century England. Juries of today are taken to be the ultimate guarantors of justice for the individual, as evinced by the strong public reaction to government plans to diminish their scope. Chosen at random from the local community, they ensure that the defendant is judged not by a remote authority, not by a civil servant, but by his own peers, people close at hand, familiar with his culture, habits and environment.

What applies to the law and legal procedures applies equally to the key players in the process. It was the community of barristers gathered together in their four Inns of Court – Gray's, Lincoln's, Inner and Middle Temple - who, more than anyone else, have evolved the English law over five centuries. Nothing illustrates better the characteristics of continuity, self-reliance, autonomy from central authority and individual responsibility than the Inns of Court: the nursery of legal talent, the fount of law and the mainstay of British justice.

Although judges in this country are appointed by the Lord Chancellor who is very much part of the government of the day, they differ in two fundamentals from their continental counterparts. They will have been barristers in private practice with years of experience at the bar and, once appointed, they are virtually autonomous from government, parliament and crown. It is fair to mention that this absolute autonomy is under threat from the Blair government with its intended abolishing of the Lord Chancellor's office along with other half-baked reforms of the recent past and promised for the imminent future.

The autonomy vested in individual judges, either acting alone or in small groups, is no mere matter of theory. It may result in wide variations of sentencing, in personal bias, even in judgements overruling the decision of a minister of the crown thought to have exceeded his authority. By being accorded such a degree of discretion in interpreting parliamentary legislation, judges do not merely implement the law, they effectively contribute to the making of it. And since these arbiters of the law are schooled in commercial realities, the world of crime and the debris of human passions, and are not the product of academic or bureaucratic establishments, British courts tend be less technical, more to do with the spirit rather the word of the law. Their verdicts are more informed by the merits of the case than by a strict technical interpretation of the wording.

English law was originally called *common* because it was meant to apply throughout the country. Its name, however, is very apt since it is grounded in common sense and is built round the expected behaviour of the common man. Ironically, it was a German, Rudolf von Jhering, the prominent 19th-century jurist, who defined perhaps most eloquently the contrasting character of the two legal cultures. He wrote "...the desire for logic that turns jurisprudence into legal mathematics is an error and arises from misunderstanding law. Life does not exist for the sake of concepts but concepts for the sake of life. It is not logic that is entitled to exist but what is claimed by life, social relations, by the sense of justice – and logical necessity or logical impossibility is immaterial." Incidentally, he also considered that only the Romans and the English had the character to balance conservative and progressive forces and thus allow their law to grow slowly and surely.

The object of every court of law, no matter where in the

world, is to administer justice. What justice is conceived to be, in what manner it is dispensed varies from land to land. In France, an investigating magistrate, as a functionary of the state, takes complete charge of a criminal case from day one. He has full authority to direct the police, to have suspects arrested, released or held in custody, to decide when and what information to release to the defence and effectively to control court proceedings. His mission is to discover the truth and produce a guilty party. It is left to the defence to try and prove that the accused is *not* guilty. Thus, for example, seven innocent people spent 3 years in custody quite recently in St Omer on the orders of a single investigating judge who believed mistakenly that he had uncovered an international paedophile ring.

Matters are somewhat different here. In the first instance the police investigates a crime. They have the power to arrest a suspect but within a very brief period, usually 24 hours, they have to charge or release him. The decision whether to take a case to court rests not with the police but with the Crown Prosecutor. If the case goes forward *all* information gathered by the police has to be disclosed to the defence. In court the presiding judge is independent from the crown and, in more serious cases, it is a jury of twelve *true* men and women, peers of the accused, unrelated to judge, prosecution or defence, that delivers the verdict. The defendant is presumed to be innocent unless the prosecution can prove beyond reasonable doubt that he is guilty. *Beyond reasonable doubt* – these three words whose meaning is imprecise, indefinable yet clearly understood, exemplify perfectly the English attitude to law.

The objective of British justice is not to establish the truth. It does not aim as high as that. Its more modest ambition is to give a *fair* chance to both sides in a combat resembling a mediaeval joust with all its ritual, costume, drama and uncertain outcome. Both prosecution and defence present their case in as biased a way as possible and do their level best to destroy testimony produced by the other side. The judge holds the ring and in his summing up ensures that his own view is carefully conveyed without the appearance of bias. The jury, silent witness to the proceedings, is then supposed to agree, unanimously if possible, as to innocence or guilt. Barristers on either side may be brilliant or humdrum, judges may be partial, the jury may be intelligent or dim, hard-headed or gullible, yet the process works surprisingly well.

There are miscarriages of justice of course, there are rogue verdicts and odd sentencing but on the whole justice is being done and seen to be done. If things go dreadfully wrong there are higher courts that may occasionally put things right, even if this reflects badly on the police, prosecution or the judicial system itself. Most of the verdicts overturned in the higher courts are not to do with the substance of a case but with the manner in which the case was conducted initially. The ultimate question is: *was the trial fair?*

The point of comparing the two legal traditions is not to evaluate them, it is to show a fundamental distinction: one is in pursuit of the truth, the other is interested in fairness. One is primarily concerned with the society and the state, the other is focused on the individual. One is classically concentric, the other typically eccentric. What matters, though, is that the new laws, new courts and the ever-expanding legal structures of the European Union are fashioned on the continental model. They are therefore not compatible with the way legal business is conducted in Britain.

7

Doing Business

It is an inevitable defect, that bureaucrats will
care more for routine than results
Walter Bagehot
The English Constitution

Large international companies try to standardise the
procedures of their subsidiaries. Even so, they are not
altogether immune from significant local variations in
business culture. Their subsidiaries may manufacture and
sell the same product, use the same marketing techniques
and accounting principles, yet as every international
manager will tell you, what works in one country does not
necessarily work in another. When it comes to indigenous
companies, the national characteristics are, of course,
further accentuated.

German companies, as one would expect, are well
organised. Responsibilities are clearly demarcated, formal
reporting procedures are strictly observed, everything is
meticulously planned and timetables are adhered to. Work
is taken seriously, people take pride in their occupation and
are judged in terms of their performance. As a result

German companies, products and services enjoy a well-earned reputation for reliability. Both companies and individuals tend to specialise and stay true to their particular expertise. There are few jacks-of-all-trades and a producer of mechanical toys will not, as a rule, start to produce wooden ones. Nor would a pharmacy easily broaden its merchandise to include cosmetics. The German consumer is wary of companies, shops, people who stray outside their acknowledged competence. As a consequence, it is difficult for a new enterprise, a new service or a new product to break into the market place. Negotiations with German companies are generally tough and straightforward. There is little flexibility but once an agreement is in place it tends to be observed even when circumstances change. If the German business culture has a weakness, it is its extreme rigidity. Lines of specialisation, of hierarchy and of function are drawn with wonderful finality. Practices, routines, rules are set in stone and it takes a huge effort of will and time to change them.

French consumers are most demanding. They are quite specific in what they want and are instinctively aware of the price/value equation. On the whole, buyers are prepared to pay a significantly higher price for a quality product, beautifully presented. France has a raft of small to medium sized companies catering for niche markets. Choice is abundant, craftsmen still survive and whatever is produced is made with an eye to detail. Generally, French people are hard-working and responsible. They also know their rights. These rights have a tendency to multiply and once bestowed, in practice, can never be removed. Backed by a never-ending flow of state-generated rules and regulations, and the innate French love of complexity, they make the conducting of any business unusually difficult.

To fully register a new company and start trading in France takes about 12 weeks and £7,000. In Britain it takes 2 days and £200. No bank anywhere likes to support start-ups at the best of times but French banks are not allowed to lend any money, even against personal guarantees, to companies before having sight of a full year's audited trading figures. Employing staff is a very serious matter. Social taxes are onerous and dismissing an employee is akin to divorce proceedings. French customs are the most vigilant and active in Europe and if they are of a mind to prevent the import of any goods into the country, with or without government prompting, they can easily do so by producing paperwork of an intricacy way beyond the comprehension of foreign exporters.

Very few tourists realise that the state officially categorises all French hotels according to the quality of service and facilities they provide. The classes range from five star to one star, as in other countries, but uniquely, there are a further 26 separate alphabetic classifications from A to Z. The distinction between a class S hotel and a class T hotel may be a tad too subtle for a guest, they are real enough to be enforceable by the inspectors of the French state. However, perhaps the most distinctive feature of French business culture is their approach to sealed and signed agreements. Whereas in other countries such agreements are considered as final, in France they are regarded merely as a framework, a starting point for the next round of negotiations. The French are past masters at composing and interpreting the small print.

As for Italy, business life is chaotic but often highly enjoyable. The Italian relish of bargaining, their natural warmth, their passion infused into the argument gives proceedings an air of drama lacking in more northern climes. One slight drawback is the notorious difficulty of extracting payment in Italy from anyone at any time. Somehow the money owed is elusive, very often late in arriving and sometimes just out of reach.

One hears a great many complaints by British businessmen as to red tape, lack of bank support, statutory minimum wages, excessive national insurance contributions and trade restrictions of all sorts. Many of these complaints are justified, yet for all that, the business climate here, relative to the rest of the continent, encourages enterprise, development of new ideas, dramatic changes in trading patterns and mobility of labour. These traits are even more pronounced in the US of course, but a certain degree of moderation has always been a feature of the British scene. Asked to sum up British business culture in a word or two, the expression *easy going* comes immediately to mind. Deals are concluded by word of mouth and set in motion; the paper work follows on later, often after the transaction itself is complete. This rather informal manner of proceeding implies a degree of mutual trust and a willingness to take quick personal decisions. Such trust placed in someone's word may not be as absolute as that between solicitors before exchanging documents but it engenders sufficient confidence to move business along, on the whole, at a much faster rate than on the continent.

The downside of such informality is easily traced in miscommunications, misunderstandings, irregular or late deliveries, faulty products, supply of wrong components, compounded errors and bits of sloppiness that litter all sectors of British commerce and industry. They contribute heavily to the general inefficiency; they cost dear in terms of time, effort and money. Statistic after statistic show Britain's productivity lagging significantly behind that of her major rivals on the continent. This weakness is usually attributed to inferior investment in research, plant, machinery and technology. The answer may well lie, at least partly, elsewhere: a job that has to be done twice, halves productivity and too many jobs have to be repeated more than once. It would appear that Britain has succeeded, over a century or so, in creating a caring and careless society. The great redeeming feature of this business culture is the wonderful response to a deadline or an emergency. Companies, and individuals within them, will pull out all the stops, work weekends and nights and coordinate their effort superbly, once they realise that someone is in real trouble and needs help.

At the end of the day what holds this eccentric, ramshackle structure together is an underlying sense of fair play. It is difficult for someone not personally involved in the life of the business community to appreciate the all-pervasive presence of this peculiarly British instinct. If someone has given you yeoman service, you do not give your business to his competitor for a slender increase in margins. You do not maximise your profits by squeezing your suppliers to death. You do not take advantage of business partners when they are struggling. There is a give and take between employer and employee; they seldom resort to the letter of a written contract. You try to resolve conflicts by a compromise both sides can live with. Of course not everyone tries to be fair, but the great majority do. Those who do not, are clearly recognised as bastards, and bastards abound all over the world. Significantly, most of the business success stories here are peopled by men not noted for their ruthlessness. British business will always compete less on organisation, efficiency, punctuality and quality, and more on its readiness to get on with the job, on flexibility, speed and individual human attitudes.

These observations may seem overly subjective to people not personally involved in commercial transactions across the continent. Fortunately a mass of statistical evidence is available to corroborate views widely held within the international business community. The World Bank publishes an annual report on doing business, country by country, surveying the international scene. A key feature of their study measures the degree of flexibility in hiring and firing employees, in conditions of employment and employment laws. Taking a combined index we find Britain on 122, fourth in world rankings, behind Singapore, the US and Denmark whilst France on 200 and Germany on 205 trail a long way behind. Another indicator measures the degree of complexity in procedures to resolve payment disputes. Here again Britain comes near the top of the list with a score of 36 whilst France with a score of 79 is the 129th country out of 133, just beating Guatemala, Sri Lanka, Panama and Venezuela.

The World Bank survey draws an important distinction between five legal traditions of regulatory regimes: those of Nordic origins, those of common-law countries, those within the German sphere of influence, those inherited from the Soviet Union and those prevalent in the Francophone world. Its comments are most pertinent: "England developed a common-law tradition, characterised by independent judges and juries, the low importance of regulation, and a preference for private litigation as a means of addressing social problems. France, following the Romans, developed civil-law tradition, characterized by state-employed judges, emphasis on legal and procedural regulation over private litigation...Nordic and common-law countries regulate the least. This finding is especially striking for the common-law group, which includes poor countries like Ethiopia, Ghana, Nigeria, Sierra Leone and Zimbabwe. Regulation is lighter in countries with more representative governments, more openness to competition, and greater political rights and media freedoms...Common-law and Nordic countries offer the best practices in business regulations. Regardless of how indices are constructed, those countries regulate the least and protect property rights the most. By combining modest levels of regulation with property rights that are clearly defined and well protected, the countries achieve what many others strive to do: have regulators act as public servants and not public masters."

The 10 least regulated countries in the world are: Australia, Canada, Denmark, Netherlands, New Zealand, Norway, Singapore, Sweden, Britain and the US. Measured by the criteria of entry procedures, employment laws, contract procedures and court powers, the most severe and rigid tradition in the world operates in the Francophone region. The dichotomy between eccentric and concentric societies, and its relevance to the European debate, can scarcely find a more clear-cut expression.

8

Language

The Oxford English Dictionary *recorded
90,000 new words and new meanings
of old words over the 20th-century*

Of all the formative influences in the development of an
individual mind, language ranks as one of the most
important. Our cognitive faculty, our learning process,
thinking habits and the way we communicate are all
conditioned by our mother tongue. Some psychologists
believe language precedes thought and no thought is
possible without it. English academic philosophy in the
second half of the last century was mostly engaged in an
attempt to reduce the great, age-old philosophical issues to
variations in the use of language and meaning of words. Be
that as it may, it is not in question that each language has
a bearing on the thinking and culture of the people born
and bred in it. Simultaneously, language is formed and
modified by the thinking and culture of the people using it.
It is a mutually reinforcing dynamic: people make a
language and language makes a people. It is thus possible,
even rewarding, to trace essential differences between

Hellenic and Hebrew character by the comparative study of the two ancient languages.

French, German, Spanish, Italian and English are all great European languages. Each has a vast vocabulary, a body of literature without compare, a rich texture and culture of its own. Fortunate are the few able to enjoy Stendhal, Thomas Mann, Lorca, Dante and Shakespeare all in the original. In terms of sound, construction, grammar and usage, they also exhibit, of course, profound differences. In origins, German, French, Italian and Spanish are pure bred. English is a mongrel tongue. The major European languages have each a single principal root whereas English has multiple ones. The capacity to ingest great chunks of other languages, to add words rather than replace them, to modify meanings, to simplify grammar, is what gives English its richness, openness and flexibility. Old Norse, Norman, Latin, French have all been made welcome and contributed hugely to a language still evolving today.

Compared to the fine, sophisticated German and French grammars, the English one is rudimentary. Perhaps, it is more helpful to ignore its rules, such as they are, than to observe them. The distinction between the use of the perfect and imperfect past, for example, seems at first sight to be reasonably straightforward. Only after decades of study does the unfortunate student of English realise that trying to apply the fine distinction between a closed, definite action and one with continuing relevance to decide which past to use, is hopeless. "I have been to Oxford" refers to a casual visit, "I was at Oxford", on the other hand, is said by someone with a lifetime of high career expectation. There are, in any case, many overlaps where the use of either form is technically correct, although using one is good English, using the other is odd. It takes an age to learn that the natives prefer to use the imperfect past whenever at all possible. Perhaps for the people of this island the past is never done and dusted, perhaps they are unwilling ever to leave it behind.

If short on grammar, English more than makes up for it in the richness of its expressions, colloquial phrases, and the array of multiple meanings of words. You can *run* in a race, *run* for office, *run* a department, *run* hell for leather, *run* yourself into the ground, *run* off, *run* up a bill, *run* down a rival, *run* down the road, *run* down leads in a criminal investigation, live in a *run*-down neighbourhood, *run* errands, *run* amok, *run* riot, *run* headlong into a brick wall, *run* scared, *run* away, *run* into trouble, *run* into debt, *run* foul of the law, *run* yourself ragged, *run* rings round your boss, be on the *run*, have a good *run* with the bat, have a *run* of bad luck, have a *run*-in with the police; a story can *run* to five pages, a death toll can *run* into hundreds, the expenditure may well *run* over the budget, and this sentence may *run* and *run*. No other language behaves in such a fashion. It makes the learning of English an arduous undertaking and mastery, for someone not born and bred to it, a truly outstanding achievement.

The German predilection for abstract nouns and the combining of them into elongated single words with a few prefixes and suffixes appended, makes the language cumbersome, heavy and precise. The habit of compressing many phrases into every sentence and the relegation of the verb to its very end, the absence of room for varied interpretations, gives the language the characteristic rigidity and stiffness associated with the people who live by it. Of the German's attitude to language one cannot say much more than that they take it very seriously. Germany today is the natural home of games. Families and friends are still wont to sit around a table, playing innovative board games, and not just at Christmas. For every card player in Britain, there are six in France and twelve in Germany. The annual winner of the Game of the Year award sells half a million copies. The Essen game fair attracts 300,000 adults and children who spend a whole day playing and trying out new games. But when it comes to word games, Germany comes a long way behind France and Britain. Her language is clearly not for fun.

The wide choice of tenses and refined syntax makes French the perfect language to convey all the subtlety and sophistication expected of her people. In its written form it is the idiom for the finest nuances of meaning, for the exact locating of the perfect phrase, the ideal word. In its spoken form it has a polished, free-flowing, dramatic attribute. The French love and guard their language jealously. New words are not simply allowed to slip into correct usage; they are admitted, if admitted at all, after years of consideration and debate, by no less august an institution than the Academie Française, the guardian of linguistic purity. When it comes to serious writing in whatever domain, academic, administrative, literary, public or private, adherence to format, elegance of style, correctness of syntax, are at least as important as the content itself. In everyday life one has the distinct impression that the French are not only fluent and articulate but that they also take pleasure in the physical act of speaking. They are understandably impatient and irritated when they are forced to hear foreigners mangle what they hold so dear.

Among languages, as a creative medium, English has no rival. It is fluid, flexible, permissive and receptive to innovation. The same word may act as a noun or a verb, a noun or an adjective, a verb or an adjective. For instance, the verb *to party* has just come into common use. The order of words within a sentence is variable. The rules of grammar and syntax are not applied too strictly. The meaning of words is liable to change without prior notice, new meanings evolve quickly and spontaneously in actual usage. Words and expressions are coined constantly and become part of the language with remarkable ease. Sometimes these coinages may be unfortunate (*humanitarian disaster*, for example, happens to be a contradiction in terms) but mostly they work well and enrich the language. *Spin doctor, topless, hands on, user friendly, cold call,* are some recent additions. The *Oxford English Dictionary* recorded 90,000 new words and new meanings of old words over the 20th-century. Although not all these words and meanings survive, it is still a staggering rate of linguistic innovation.

All languages transport words and expressions from one sphere to another but none of them on anything like the scale in English. Take the world of sport: *level playing field, kick into touch, dubious call, sticky wicket, good innings, move the goal posts, be stumped for an answer, tackle a job, blow the whistle, long odds, field questions, the rub of the green, bunkered, a good pitch, the ball is in your court,* are just some of expressions in everyday use that began life there. Lateral thinking is part of the genius of the language.

Even as late as the 14th-century written English was an underground language. It grew its literary grass roots against powerful opposition from central authority:

Oxbridge, Church and Court. The two creative giants who helped to embed the language were both poets: William Tyndale with his contribution to the inspired language of the King James Bible and Shakespeare, of course, with the power and incomparable richness of his art. That they should be poets is no coincidence, for English is, above all others, the language of poetry. Poetic use of language, in essence, gives words and phrases unconventional associations, original contexts, multiple resonance, unexpected meanings. English is just made for it.

Unlike the French and the Germans, Brits do not treat their language with a great deal of respect. They are hesitant and sloppy in speech, careless in writing. Even in the academic world good use of English now counts for little. Schools do not pay much attention to correct spelling or grammar and do not nurture vital writing skills; they do not even aim to produce intelligible diction. Miscommunication is the order of the day. On the other hand, the majority of the people are into crosswords and a vast variety of other word games that feature regularly on the television and in the press. Play on the multiple meaning of words and phrases is one of the main sources of a stream of humour that is never vast enough to quench this nation's comic appetite.

The inherent structural characteristics of English and those of the principal continental languages differ profoundly. So do the relationships of the people to their own language. These differences underlie and reflect a crucial distinction between eccentric and concentric cultures that no one can afford to ignore.

9

Philosophy

Common sense is very rare
Voltaire

Philosophy, as the term is widely understood, is concerned with universal truths, truths that transcend the boundaries of time and place, of language and national culture. But philosophers live in a given era and their work both reflects and modifies the specific culture they inhabit. It is not the validity of their argument, not the brilliance of their ideas, not the quality of their logic that interests us here but the differences between the cultures of which they are a part.

Plato and Aristotle could be said to be the founding fathers of two fundamentally contrasting philosophic traditions. Plato considered the mundane, everyday world of objects and creatures as a mere pale, imperfect shadow of another kind of world, a world of ideas, of perfection, a world we cannot touch or see. Aristotle, on the other hand, focused his attention on the tangible world, on what we can observe, study, classify, compare, define and analyse. Aristotle's method eventually leads to the sciences, Plato's thinking introduces us to the splendours of metaphysics.

This distinction, as it so happens, illustrates accurately a profound contrast between continental and English philosophers. The work of, for example, Leibnitz, Descartes, Spinoza, Kant, Hegel, Husserl, Schopenhauer, Kierkegaard, is in every case founded on a big idea, or a set of big ideas. Each one aspires to an absolute truth, to a final resolution of fundamental questions about the universe and man's place within it. Often critical of preceding philosophies and sometimes difficult to follow, they are nevertheless magnificent, indeed majestic edifices of pure, speculative thought. Like Plato's writings, they unfold seamlessly from a central core of original ideas in a series of brilliant insights, retaining the logical coherence of a self-contained, systematic whole. Nothing comparable has ever emerged in the history of English philosophy.

True to the Aristotelian tradition, English philosophers, with the possible exception of Bishop Berkeley, who was Irish anyway, have set themselves more modest goals. Francis Bacon, Hobbes, Locke, Hume, John Stuart Mill, all grounded their thoughts in easily observable realities. They tried to accommodate mundane particulars into broader, more general principles, principles borne out by experience, even the experience of the philosophically untrained, ordinary man. In their speculative thinking they seldom strayed beyond that which could be related back to their tangible starting point. If the outcome of philosophical thought came into conflict with everyday experience, then, for them, there was no contest: the reality in front of our eyes won every time.

As with epistemology, which is concerned with theories of knowledge, so with ethics: the same distinction holds true. In considering the ultimate principles of morality,

Kant formulates the Categorical Imperative of Practical Reason: "Act only on that maxim through which you can at the same time will that it should become a universal law." Applied to human relationships the Imperative becomes: "So act as to treat humanity, whether in your own person or that of any other, as an end in himself, never as means only." How striking, how inspiring, how Teutonic. Who would have thought in Britain to turn the local practice of treating other human beings with *common decency* into the theoretical foundation of a moral philosophy? It is a great shame though that the Categorical Imperative was not much in evidence in Germany when millions of Jews were reduced to soap.

In contrast, Hobbes and Locke base their ideas of a "social contract" on a practical assessment of human nature, characterised primarily by self-interest and self-assertion, which has to be curbed to allow for the functioning of society. Even though Mill dilutes the stark utilitarian principle of "the greatest happiness or pleasure of the greatest number" and develops ideas of "the social feelings of mankind: the desire to be in unity with our fellow creatures", he does not raise unrealistic expectations as to man's noble instincts and unselfish self-sacrifice. He considers men not so much as they ought to be but as they really are.

In a nutshell, English philosophic tradition leans towards empirical evidence, prefers a pragmatic approach and, above all, draws heavily on the archetypical British characteristic of *common sense*. On the continent the tendency has been to proceed from abstract first principles, construct coherent systems and accommodate perceived reality within a logical, unified universe. It is aesthetically more satisfying, though practically less relevant.

Political life in this country has never taken kindly to intellectuals and academics, has been wary of principles and theories, and suspicious of revolutionary ideas above all. Perhaps this is because if and when such theories and ideas wander from the academic domain into the political arena, the outcome is not guaranteed to be desirable. The descents from the principles of *Liberté, Egalité, Fraternité* to the guillotine, from Hegel's dialectical materialism to practical communism and the Gulags of Siberia, from the noble vision of Nietzsche's Superman to crude racial ideologies and the holocaust, are only too slippery.

Bold and great ideas, nourish all civilisations. Without them the human race could not have accomplished much. But ideas, once embodied in the real world, are not without peril. In concentric political cultures, in the hands of a powerful centre, applied from above at a forced pace, they can prove disastrous. In the eccentric British climate, ideas are absorbed gradually, they percolate down many channels of social and commercial activity and are heavily diluted by practical experience before their adoption as integral parts of any political reality. A Greater Europe is a very big idea indeed. The question is this: should it be imposed from the top or will it be allowed to grow, if the idea is intrinsically strong enough, from the ground up? The answer to this question determines whether concentric or eccentric forces will win the struggle for the future of the continent.

10

Sense of Humour

*There is more Humour in our English Comick writers
than in any others. I do not wonder at it, for I look
upon Humour to be almost of English Growth;
at least, it does not seem to have found such
Encrease on any other Soil*
William Congreve

Humour is not a laughing matter. At least not just a
laughing matter. Freud was not the only thinker to
highlight the function of the comic element in our lives. We
find traces of it early in the Old Testament where Isaac (the
laughing one) was so named because Sarah, his mother,
found the prediction that she would bear a child at the age
of ninety, quite amusing. The comedies of Aristophanes
were at least as popular as the tragedies of Sophocles. Every
self-respecting court in medieval Europe had its jester
whose purpose in life was to mock everyone and give voice
to the unmentionable. The very vocabulary of humour is
extensive: farce, slapstick, satire, irony, parody, comedy,
caricature, clowning, joke, jest, quip, repartee, wit, to list a
few.

But what has this to do with the weighty matter of European integration? Only this: national cultures have significantly differing volumes of comic content. On the whole, cultures with a rich vein of humour tend to be eccentric, those less well endowed have distinctly concentric inclinations. This is to be expected. Humour, in essence, is irreverent. It challenges convention, the establishment, icons and taboos, in the home, at school, at work, in government, everywhere. It has proved to be a potent form of defence against overbearing authority.

Through my origins, I am schooled in Hungarian and Jewish humour. Of all the Hungarian industries, the manufacturing of jokes is the most prolific. The variety, the degree of sophistication, the originality of Hungarian jokes is perhaps unsurpassed. On my frequent trips to the country during the communist era, every encounter, private or business, began with a series of freshly minted jokes, often told by party members and officials, invariably against the regime, invariably vicious. The temptation to poke fun at those who made rational life impossible was just too strong. Incidentally, Hungary also produced one of the great writers of the comic genre in Karinthy Frigyes, whose profound humour is alas lost in translation. His compatriot, George Mikes, inspired by the Master, had the good fortune to write in English and so his works, notably *How to be an Alien* and *Shakespeare and I*, had a much wider audience. Jewish humour, at its best, has great depth. It has certain analogies with the Negro spiritual, music likewise created by people living in a hostile environment, resigned yet defiant, introspective, using a language of their own to the exclusion of outsiders. Jewish humour is mostly a wry commentary on life by Jews, for Jews, about Jews.

You have to be a Jew to appreciate it.

Literary masterpieces of humour are found in many languages. The Italians have Boccaccio's *Decameron*, the Spanish have Cervantes' *Don Quixote*, Moliére and Voltaire adorn French, *The Good Soldier Svejk* was written in Czech and Gogol's *The Government Inspector* is a Russian classic. Even the Germans can boast a rare sample in Thomas Mann's *Felix Krull*. But enter the realms of English literature and the floodgates open. Chaucer, Shakespeare, Congreve, Swift, Sterne, Sheridan, Dickens, Thackeray, Trollope, Lewis Carroll, Edward Lear, Kipling, Jerome K. Jerome, Oscar Wilde, George Bernard Shaw, A.A. Milne, Woodhouse, Orwell and so, endlessly, on. If the volume is staggering, so is the range. The brilliant wordplay of *Love's Labour Lost*, the metaphor of Gulliver, the crude farce of Restoration plays, the gently hilarious *Pickwick Papers*, the social satire of *Vanity Fair*, the surreal world of Alice, the nonsense of Lear, the prankish schoolboy world of *Stalkey & Co*, the wit and repartee of Wilde, the ingenuity of *Pygmalion*, the adult dimension of *Winnie the Pooh*, the pathos of *The Diary of a Nobody*, the savage allegory of *Animal Farm*, all represent quite distinct strains in a living universe of humour that permeates English literary genius. Remarkably, the writer of comedies and tragedies, comic and epic tales, light hearted and grim fiction, is often the selfsame author. *Macbeth* and *Midsummer Night Dream* flow from the same pen, so do *Bleak House* and *The Pickwick Papers*, so do *It* and *Stalkey & Co*, and the man who created *Animal Farm* also wrote *1984*.

The flow of humour inundated every branch of the emerging new media. During the war Tommy Handley's radio show, *ITMA*, helped to keep the nation's spirits alive. He was followed by *The Goon Show*, breeding ground for the comic genius of Spike Milligan and Peter Sellers. *Beyond Our Ken* and *Hancock's Half Hour* became radio classics, each in its own distinctive style. On TV, drawing on the tradition of stand up comedy, Tommy Cooper, Frankie Howerd, Ken Dodd, Morecombe and Wise, all established original comic formats and became household icons. On cinema screens, the Ealing comedies, *The Lavender Hill Mob*, *Kind Hearts and Coronets*, *Passport to Pimlico*, *The Ladykillers* set new standards and helped establish Alec Guinness as one of the all time greats. The *Carry On* series, of lesser quality but of broader appeal, went on for many years. Inspector Clouzot exported Peter Sellers' brand of lunacy all over the world. But it is television that provides the richest yield: *Steptoe and Son*, *'Allo 'Allo*, *Monty Python*, *Dad's Army*, *Some Mothers Do 'Ave 'Em*, *Yes Minister*, *Till Death Do Us Part*, *The Good Life*, *Keeping Up Appearances*, *Fawlty Towers*, *One Foot In The Grave*, *Only Fools and Horses*, all minor classics, all likely to pass the test of time.

This is all familiar to people living here, who have come to expect this flow, in the theatre, on television, in fiction, to be inexhaustible. What is less well known is how it compares with the humour content of other cultures. Since relatively few English speakers bother with foreign languages and since humour as an essential part of life is taken for granted, the assumption is that other nations have similar taste buds and hunger for humour, the same discernment, the same variety and riches. Nothing could be further from the truth.

If English humour is taken to be a sea, other cultures

may at best possess a modest lake while the less fortunate have perhaps a garden pond. Roughly the same proportions apply when it comes to quality, variety, originality, sophistication and depth. Laughing is part of human nature; people of all nations find things occasionally funny and develop their own comic dimension; but nowhere else in the world does humour form so essential or all-pervasive a part of daily life. It is one of the defining qualities of the British character. In adversity, stress, frustration, disappointment, when fighting hopeless odds, there is always that comical turn of phrase, that joke, that amusing remark to release tension, elicit laughter, gain breathing space, and so allow a more detached view to be taken of an apparent catastrophe. Unlike elsewhere, humour in these parts knows no boundaries and is not confined to specific occasions. It bubbles constantly beneath the surface liable to erupt anywhere at any time. It respects no person, institution, office, class, race, religion, tradition, icon and especially no authority. No one, or nothing is immune. Some of it is weak, some is in poor taste, much of it smutty, some of it over the top and some of it offends. But, for better or worse, it is omnipresent.

The means of managing people are limited: setting targets, making promises or demands, giving orders, asking for help, employing charm, inspiration, threats, persuasion, argument, manipulation and, finally, humour. I have had to work with people of many different nationalities and tried, at one time or other, the lot. Since I find humour instinctive it has become a natural ingredient of what communication skills I have managed to evolve. It works better in some places than others. The ease of eliciting a response has become, for me, a national barometer of humour. In this country it almost never fails. In Germany it almost never succeeds. This may change in the future, as I am told that managers of Lufthansa, Daimler-Chrysler and other major corporations now attend three-day seminars to acquire the secrets of "winning humour" as a management tool. No doubt "organised, systematic spontaneity" is next on the list.

Political satire is just one, and by no means the most interesting, of the many comic elements that define a nation's humour. The cabarets of pre-Nazi Berlin have not lacked an audience, the magazine *Le Canard Enchaîné* has a substantial following in France nowadays while political cartoons, mostly nation specific, are ubiquitous in Europe. But its roots are deeper and its fruits more prolific in England. Political life in 18th-century Britain cannot be understood without reference to the paper-trail of satirical cartoons and lampoons that hounded party leaders and royalty alike. George III was driven to such distraction by the pen of John Wilkes that he had the man locked up in the Tower. Not that it did the King any good; wounding pamphlets continued to flow unabated. James Gillray's cartoons were particularly effective against Whig circles around Charles James Fox, so sympathetic to the French Revolution. Most of us have witnessed the effect of programmes like *That Was The Week That Was, Spitting Image, Have I Got News For You*, as well as the biting satire of the daily Press and the fortnightly *Private Eye*, on political figures of this generation. Being in the public eye nowadays is akin to navigating a minefield. A sex scandal, financial manipulation, being caught in an embarassing lie, or an unfortunate choice of friends, all can blow a career sky high. To be put to ridicule is a subtler, more prolonged, more painful form of execution. This is why politicians in this country perhaps dread it most.

Governing democracies has never been easy. In a world where simplified images and sound bites have often displaced serious debate, the corrosive effect of humour makes the life of leaders doubly difficult. This is the price an eccentric society pays in terms of political efficacy. Obviously, Britain, the most eccentric of all working democracies, has found the price worth paying.

11

Multicultural Society

*I believe that political correctness can be a form of
fascism, and it sends shivers down the spine of my
generation, who went to war against fascism*

P.D. James

Whether we like it or not, national traits exist. They
differentiate people, they are profound and they change, if
at all, over many, many generations. The proponents of a
Greater Europe respond to this uncomfortable reality with
characteristic idealism: do these differences matter, they
ask? Is not the cultural diversity of Europe a splendid
thing? Will not these very differences produce the dynamic
tensions so essential for bringing about much needed
reform? Will not each nation, with its own culture,
contribute something special to the new mix? Will not these
widely differing cultures cross fertilise each other and so
give birth to a new political reality, superior to anything
ever seen before? A single, cohesive multicultural
continent?

The recently coined term *multicultural society* trips
lightly off the tongue. It goes well with *multilingual,*

multilateral, multifunctional. These terms have clear and unambiguous meanings; *multicultural* has neither. Contrary to the opinion of Robin Cook, the amount of Chicken Tikka Masala consumed in Britain is no indication of the emergence of a multicultural society hereabouts, any more than the quantities of pizzas we eat or French wine we drink. Not even the presence of minority ethnic groups – African, Caribbean, Hindu or others, immigrants that, initially at least, retain some of their native culture – justifies such a label. For many centuries, British society has accepted, absorbed and assimilated many culturally distinct immigrant groups, such as the Huguenots, the Jews, the Irish and more recently the West Indians, without relinquishing its own single culture status. Certainly the key to the success of the United States, so far, has been its capacity to assimilate each generation of newcomers to its own, basically Anglo-Saxon culture, a culture that has been evolving there for over three hundred years.

If the concept of a multicultural entity has a meaning, it must apply to countries without a single dominant culture, or to those *blessed* with a number of competing ones. Northern Ireland, the Ottoman Empire, the Austro-Hungarian Empire, Yugoslavia, Canada and Belgium may be so termed and they do not have a great track record. The Ottoman Empire, Austro-Hungary and Yugoslavia are gone, Northern Ireland awaits a painful resolution, Quebec seems to be a permanently unresolved issue poisoning the body politic of Canada, while the political cohabitation of Flemish and Walloon cultures in Belgium is a most unhappy one. As someone born and bred in Transylvania, where Romanian, Hungarian, German and Jewish cultures lived for many uneasy years cheek by jowl, I would not recommend the voluntary creation of such a political framework. Perhaps multicultural societies should not be viewed as objects of political aspiration but as tragic ethnographic accidents.

There is such a thing as a common European heritage even if it may not be easy to define it with any precision. National cultures within Europe have significantly influenced each other in all spheres, from the humble habits of eating and drinking to the most exalted forms of classical music and fine art. The Renaissance has left no corner of the continent unaffected, the Reformation respected no national frontiers, the fairy tales of Hans Christian Andersen are familiar to virtually every European child, Champagne is now synonymous with celebration everywhere. In fact, these cultural cross currents are a vital part of a cohesive continent and they are essential elements in any attempt at creating a common European enterprise, like, for example, the Common Market. Hence, we have to be very careful in trying to understand how these individual cultures operate and interact.

Cultural phenomena are firmly rooted within a nation or region long before they are transmitted further afield. The Renaissance becomes a powerful movement in Florence before its waves transform a continent. Martin Luther lives and preaches in Wittenberg, and so his teachings go forth from a well-established base in Germany. Andersen's tales are told in his native Danish and much later translated into other European languages. Centuries of wine-making tradition in the geographical area of Champagne precede its intoxicating march across the world.

When a tradition, an idea or a structure, in whatever sphere, moves from one culture to another, it moves *not* by decree, *not* by any kind of consensus, *not* by planned inter-governmental agreement, but unpredictably, by its own volition, in response to the spontaneous welcome of the recipient culture. Traditions, ideas, institutions cannot be imported successfully by *decisions*, democratic or despotic, unless there is a natural attraction for them. More importantly, cultural imports are almost invariably modified in the process, emerging as modified versions of the originals. The Renaissance in the Northern countries produced its own art and architecture some way distant from its Florentine counterpart. The British model of constitutional monarchy has reappeared in many iterations, some more constitutional than others, throughout Europe from the eighteenth century onwards. The Sichuan dishes served in Chinese restaurants, so pleasing to a Western palate, hardly correspond to the simple, austere cooking of the largest province of China.

National traits are much more than a haphazard collection of the amusing or irritating peculiarities of a given people. These very same attributes help to form their language, literature, thinking, their social habits, attitudes, laws, business propensities, political institutions, their art and architecture. In short, they are what underpin a national culture. This culture in turn further reinforces the national traits that have gone into the making of it. It all hangs together. In order to safeguard the valuable cultural cross currents within Europe, it is essential, therefore, to preserve the integrity of individual nations where traditions, ideas and institutions are naturally spawned. It is vital to allow the movement between cultures to be free and spontaneous rather than structured and politically superimposed. It is imperative to allow each nation to adapt any cultural import to its own existing structures, institutions, temperament and tradition. In the final analysis, European culture is inimical to, and incompatible with, a multicultural Europe.

The idea of fairness, of fair play, for example, is omnipresent in British culture. It is there in the worlds of sport, business, law, entertainment, even politics. One of the first refrains of children against the edicts of their elders is that they are unfair. The habitual parental response, namely that *life is unfair*, merely reinforces an ideal, difficult to attain in practice. Significantly, the word *fair* does not translate. No other language has an equivalent. The nearest terms are *just* or *reasonable*, but they are nowhere near the same. When perhaps the single most influential term in a culture is missing from the vocabulary of neighbouring ones, any idea of inter-marriage should give rise to a long pause for thought.

To ignore profound differences in national traits, to try to separate culture from nationhood, to abstract any part of a national culture and attempt artificially to merge it with national cultures alien to it, is not only futile but counterproductive. Clearly, in terms of institutions, constitutions, history, traditions and practices, political culture varies widely within Europe. The very nature of democracy itself is far from being the same across the continent. It follows, therefore, that the deliberate and conscious effort to pursue a course leading to the political integration of Europe is perilous and ultimately doomed to failure. It is doomed to failure because of the irreconcilable nature of the differences in national traits and cultures. It is perilous because in their tactical haste, the politicians of integration will create havoc all around and delay a much slower but natural coming together of the European peoples.

12

A New Constitution
The Road Map to a Greater Europe

"Where I use a word" Humpty Dumpty said,
in a rather scornful tone,
"it means just what I chose it to mean -
neither more nor less"
Lewis Carroll
Through the Looking Glass

The Convention on the Future of Europe has completed its work. The final draft of a new Constitution, all 465 clauses of it (that of the US has 33), in 21 different languages, was officially handed over to the subscribing national governments in Rome on July 17th 2003. The Inter-Governmental Conference has now approved the text with minor modifications and Britain is set to ratify a new, comprehensive European Constitution. The head of the Convention, Giscard d'Estaing, was French, which is as it should be. After all, the French promulgated so many constitutions over the last two centuries that drafting them has become something of a routine. Guided by logic and permeated with noble ideas, none of them proved durable in practice. If that of the Fifth Republic fails, the Sixth Republic will have an improved version.

Tony Blair, most reluctantly, promised in principle to consult the British people by submitting the proposed constitution to a referendum. The public debate leading to the referendum will divide the country into two opposing camps: those who want an ever tighter integration of Europe and those who are against additional transfer of powers to the EU. The discussion is likely to focus on the meaning and implications of specific articles of the Constitution and the small print of certain paragraphs within it, to demonstrate the threat, or its absence, to British independence. Such an analysis is, of course, of vital importance to the nation. If the debate is thus confined there is a danger that it will degenerate into competing semantics and leave the lay public confused and bored by a subject that is not exactly the bread and butter of everyday life. It is important therefore to place this entire constitutional exercise in a wider context: how did it come about, what is its purpose, who drove it and why has it assumed this particular form. The answers to these questions also illustrate, incidentally, just how political business is conducted in Europe.

A European constitution, what for? It is a legitimate question to ask since Britain has managed her affairs tolerably well thus far without a written constitution. There has been no noticeable public demand for such a constitution anywhere on the continent, no street demonstrations, no media campaigns, no pressure groups.

Trade unions, chambers of commerce, professional bodies, courts of law, have not asked for it and the subject was not even debated, never mind voted on, in any of the national parliaments. In extensive travels through many countries, discussing the topic of the EU over the last few years, no one ever suggested that what Europe needed above all else was a brand new constitution. So if it is not demanded by the people, then who inspires it, drives it, needs it? No great surprises here. It is the same political establishment that is engaged in constructing the new reality of a Greater Europe. The EU has an integrated economy, an administrative centre, a supreme court of law, a common currency, a central bank, a flag, so why not a constitution? It is the next logical step and a great deal easier to accomplish than joint armed forces and a federal government. Those can follow later, in due course.

The constitution of a state, as the term suggests, is meant to define its legal foundation. The constitution of the United States, for example, came to be written by people of separate colonies who wanted to constitute themselves into an independent, sovereign state. Their purpose was to fix for all time the principles from which no subsequent legislation and no government in power could diverge. As part of the exercise, they wanted to set in stone the minimal rights of the citizens within the new state, like the right to life, liberty and the pursuit of happiness. The central idea of any constitution, be it of a political entity or a private club, is to establish an inviolate set of rules that cannot be changed except with the consent of the population of a state, or the entire membership of a club. Thus, in theory, a government should be prevented from enforcing an unconstitutional law as the executive committee of a cricket club should be deprived of overriding the fundamental intentions of the founders. In practice, all written constitutions have a number of serious inherent flaws:

- Being timeless, a constitution's terms have to be abstract, and therefore not easy to apply to individual cases and concrete realities.
- The distinction between what touches on the constitution and what does not, is not always evident. Ambiguous instances, grey areas, often the ones that matter most, have to be referred to an independent authority.
- Being formulated all in one go, it is heavily influenced by the specific and transient circumstances prevailing at the time of its creation.
- As time passes and circumstances change, even the fundamentals may need reviewing but, being embodied in a sacrosanct document, this is a notoriously difficult process.
- Finally, being so neatly encapsulated, any determined and powerful central authority can simply scrap or rewrite it at will. Historical examples, unfortunately, are not lacking. The carefully crafted constitution of Zimbabwe has not provided much protection to the white farmers who have so recently lost all their worldly goods.

An unwritten constitution suffers none of these drawbacks. The fact that it is not embodied in a self-contained document does not mean it is any less effective. On the contrary, being implicit in parliamentary legislation and the conduct of government, being modified episodically, on a partial basis, it is more relevant, more alive and tends to endure better than its written counterpart. It may be more accurate to say that Britain has a rolling constitution rather than an unwritten one.

If written constitutions in general have inherent flaws, they are magnified in the proposed European one. Thus far in history, those drafting a constitution have been of one mind as to what it was meant to accomplish. The Founding Fathers, meeting in Philadelphia in 1787, not only had a common agenda, they also shared one language and the same political culture. This is not the case here. There have been more agendas on the table than the number of delegates engaged in drafting it. The minor states would fight for equality, irrespective of size. The larger ones, particularly France and Germany, would push for the opposite. The integrationists wanted a document that would naturally lead to a federal state, something like that of the United States. Idealists of all descriptions had the usual extensive shopping list of individual human rights crying out for inclusion. Delegates from different countries had sacred cows of their own. Apparently, Giscard's pet idea is Space, so it has found its way into the text. The governments of France, Germany, Spain, Britain and no doubt many other nations had specific, and very different, areas over which they wanted to retain national control. The Commission is congenitally bent on acquiring ever more power, increasing the scope of its authority whilst the European Parliament, in the name of democracy, will always press for greater say. Britain wanted no constitution at all, merely an updating, streamlining and the clarifying of existing treaties. Those driving the project would be satisfied with nothing less than a European Bible encapsulating the future destiny of the continent.

Every constitution written hitherto has served a single autonomous body, with its own government, laws, judiciary and the physical means to enforce the law. The proposed European constitution will apply to a political entity that has none of these. For the first time ever we have a constitution for a political entity, the EU, still theoretically subject to the higher authority of the individual national parliaments. So it will depend on the conformity of 25 or more governments, their parliaments, laws, judiciary, police and armies for its application, maintenance and continued existence. It is a classic case of putting the cart before the horse.

Thus far, the constitution of every sovereign state has been the sole one, its supremacy unchallenged. The European constitution is meant to embrace people who already have one of their own. It will have to compete with 25 other existing constitutions, unless or until all national constitutions are consigned to oblivion. More than that, this unique enterprise purports to define not just the rights as between a putative state and its citizens but also the rights as between member states and their supra-national Union, all in one comprehensive, ambitious document. But, at the end of the day, there will always be disputed cases and competing authorities. The question as to what is a constitutional issue and what is not, arises even within single states. So a European Constitutional Court, needed to adjudicate disputes between nations and the Union, would add another august institution to an already impressive list that includes the European Court of Justice, the European Court of Human Rights, the European Parliament, the European Commission, The European

Central Bank. Let us just imagine for a moment that France, despite having more than adequate representation within such a constitutional court, is found to have acted unconstitutionally. What are the remedies? What are the ultimate sanctions? Fines? Politicians jailed? Loss of rights? Expulsion? Who will enforce them? Or will France, as usual, engineer the re-writing of the relevant clause?

When the constitution needs amending or reforming, as constitutions always do, how will this be accomplished? Who will propose it? Who will accept it? Will a new Convention be appointed for any periodic review? Will the national parliaments be asked to endorse each proposed amendment? Will the proposed amendments require unanimity, simple majority or what? How will all this work? Has anyone thought through the enormous complexities, the vast areas for disagreement, the unlimited potential for conflict, the danger of disturbing those European practices that are currently working tolerably well? Some interesting questions; no easy, credible answers.

All these issues, the conflicting interests, the irreconcilable objectives, the lack of a single common vision of a future Europe, must have been clear to all the participating governments. So how did this monstrosity of a project ever get off the ground? European initiatives invariably employ a convenient trigger to set a project in motion. In this case, the enlargement of the Union, anticipating a membership of 25 states with more to come, provided the perfect opportunity for the concentric forces, both within and without Brussels, to embark on the next major phase of continental integration. The argument that the Union of 25 member states could not be expected to manage its business within the parameters of successive treaties agreed previously must have sounded reasonable. Especially so since the Laeken Declaration, that launched the constitutional exercise, promised to reduce EU bureaucracy, to simplify the rules, to bring European institutions closer to the citizens and work towards a clear, open, effective, democratically controlled Community approach. Having learnt nothing from 40 years of EU politics, the British Government, incredibly, took the Declaration at face value. Otherwise it is difficult to understand, in the light of what actually transpired, why it did not put a stop to the project before it was born.

The proceedings of the Convention were controlled by a Presidium of 13 members: Valéry Giscard d'Estaing, an outspoken integrationist; as President, Jean Luc Dehane of Belgium and Giuliano Amato of Italy, former prime ministers and avowed federalists as Vice-Presidents; two European Commissioners; two MEPs; three government representatives; a representative of new member countries and two national Parliamentarians. Various working groups were established, their recommendations were, however, subject to the discretion of the Presidium. No more objective account of how the Convention worked, of how the constitution came to be drafted, is available than the pamphlet titled "The Making of Europe's Constitution" published by the Fabian Society and written by Gisela Stuart, a member of the Presidium itself. Of German origin, a Labour MP since 1997 and strong supporter of British involvement in Europe, the author is untainted by Euro skepticism of Tory or any other variety. What she has to say on the subject is revealing:

"The extent to which national parliamentarians felt obliged to account for decisions at the Convention to their parliaments varied; those from the UK set a good example that was rarely followed elsewhere.

National parliamentarians were the visitors to Brussels, invited to meetings and used to endorse the decisions reached by European interest groups.

The Presidium was the drafting body, deciding which working groups' recommendations should be accepted almost unchanged and which should be almost ignored. The President regularly consulted with heads of government to ensure agreement by the large member states, and the Commission and The European Parliament worked closely together, easy for them as they are both based in Brussels.

Laeken had posed a number of specific questions but rather than answering them, after six months of general debates the Presidium presented the Convention members with a skeleton structure of a Constitution. Without debate, it was simply accepted that this was the most appropriate way of fulfilling the Laeken mandate.

It was at one of the dinners at Val Duchess that the skeleton of the draft constitution was given to members of the Presidium in sealed brown envelopes the weekend before the public presentation. We were not allowed to take the documents away with us. Just precisely who drafted the skeleton, and when, is still unclear to me, but I gather much of the work was done by Valéry Giscard d'Estaing and Sir

John Kerr over the summer. There was little time for informed discussion, and even less scope for changes to be made.

The secretariat was very skilful when it came to deciding which decisions of the Presidium would be reflected in subsequent papers. The agenda issued beforehand was simply indicative and the sheer mass of paper which was produced meant that large parts of the text passed through without detailed discussions.

On one occasion, a redraft of the articles dealing with defence mysteriously arrived for circulation just before midnight. They were written in French and the authorship was unclear. Verbal reassurances were given to those of us who felt uneasy about approving a legal text in an unfamiliar language, that this was little more than 'a linguistically better draft of the earlier English version'. The draft was discarded when some of us spotted that references to NATO had mysteriously disappeared.

The six founding Member States struck agreements on the Draft Constitution in last-minute deals in the Presidium. From high-minded beginnings, the Convention became a mixture of individual idiosyncrasies, principled positions and political horse-trading.

Neither could we endorse the text on behalf of the parliaments who had sent us. Yet, hardly was the ink dry on the Draft than this was turned into an endorsement by all those present and governments were warned not to open up the carefully achieved compromises. The 'consensus' reached was only among those who shared a particular view of what the Constitution was supposed to achieve.

Despite sixteen months of work and thousands of words written or spoken, it is clear that the Constitution is little understood and that the Convention did not succeed in its stated aim of involving the public at large."

These remarks give but a flavour of standard concentric political practices. Reading the pamphlet one is left with the impression that the author, brought up in British politics, must have experienced a culture shock to impel her to publish her observations, bravely jeopardizing a political career in the process. At any rate, she bears first hand witness that a narrow, highly motivated, integrationist circle ran the show and largely determined the final outcome. Consultation with "representatives of civil society", in the best French tradition, turned out to be a farcical succession of lobby groups, most of them well known within the Brussels ambit. A Youth Convention, established for the same purpose, turned out to be more independent and troublesome, so it was quietly buried. Any significant input was confined to two hugely self-interested sources: the European Parliament and the European Commission. Their common agenda has always been for each to acquire power at the expense of national parliaments.

Understanding why the Constitution came into being and how it was drafted is of some help in approaching a document that runs to some 335 pages none of which will have been read by the vast majority of voters in the forthcoming referendum. Government spin will exploit this fact by focusing attention on carefully edited assurances to demonstrate that the Constitution does not significantly change Britain's relationship to the EU. It is important to highlight therefore the general tone and intention of the exercise as well as those key provisions in the text that have a vital bearing on the development of what is beginning to resemble uncannily a European multi-state.

This Convention, in the tradition of all such conventions, brought forth an impressive sounding document. It is long on abstract principles, sacrosanct rights, vague generalities, ambiguity, unobjectionable assertions and democratic sentiment. For example: "The Union ...shall contribute to peace, security, the sustainable development of the earth, solidarity and mutual respect among peoples, free and fair trade, eradication of poverty, protection of human rights..." It is, however, short on specifics, clarity, practical distinctions, useful detail and enforceable rule. It attempts to circumvent the most difficult issues it was set up to resolve. As there could be no common ground, no unified purpose, the Presidium focused its efforts on coining a language open to multiple interpretations, on forging not a common destiny but a document based on the lowest common denominator: ease of public consumption.

From the very first page, the tone is set, the language is indicative, the mind-set unmistakable: ...*Convinced that, while remaining proud of their national identity and history, the peoples of Europe are determined to transcend their ancient divisions and, united ever more closely, to forge a common destiny.* Incidentally, the French text differs subtly: the term *national* is attached to *history* NOT to *identity*, and instead of *A common destiny*, it reads

THEIR common destiny. The French version implies that the common destiny already exists. Such elementary differences in meaning in the two texts, right at the outset, speak volumes about the whole enterprise.

For the sake of grasping the intent of the whole document it is worthwhile to dwell a little on this remarkable key statement:

First, the Presidium has no qualms about speaking in the name of all the peoples of Europe.

Second, the reference to individual states forms a sub clause and is limited to an expression of pride.

Third, identity is linked to history, something irrelevant to the present or the future. *National identity* in any case is difficult to define and carries no concrete political weight. The Scots, the Welsh, the Flemish, the Frisians all are proud of their national identity and history without having an independent state of their own.

Fourth, the principal verb in the sentence is *determined.* Not just *desirous* or *aspiring* or even *intent on*, it has to be the strongest term available. Where exactly this mass of determined humanity is manifest remains a mystery.

Fifth, the climax of the statement, with all the rest building to it, is undoubtedly the last phrase: to forge a common destiny. *Transcending ancient divisions* is vague enough. *Uniting ever more closely* is more explicit. *Forging a common destiny* is pretty serious. For if it says anything at all, it means that Britain has to swim or sink with the continent – she has no future of her own.

Sixth, the statement is most subtly crafted. The language reads well, sounds good and is aesthetically pleasing. To people in this country this may be of little significance. To those animating the political culture of the continent, particularly Giscard d'Estaing and his team of architects, it is the prime objective of the whole exercise, more important even than the federalist substance, never mind whether it is useful or workable at all. No British politician, no matter how steeped in clichés and vacuous pronouncements, would dream of uttering such pomposities. Such language is totally alien to this island.

Now, for some of the more obvious highlights:

- Preamble: *Reflecting the will of the citizens and the States of Europe to build a common future, this constitution establishes the European Union, on which member states confer competences to obtain objectives they have in common. The Union shall co-ordinate the policies by which member states aim to achieve these objectives.*

The *citizens of Europe* now appear as a distinct entity over and above the member states. The *will of the people* is an expression particularly favoured by leaders unaccustomed to consulting the people through the ballot box. *Competence*, a term much laboured throughout, means the power of decision making, not the *ability* to do so. Such subtle distortions of the common use of language, to make the text more palatable, are characteristic of the entire draft. The corresponding German text with *zustaendigkeit*, having the clear connotation of authority, is more transparent. What does "co-ordinate" exactly mean? A notoriously elastic term, it could translate to something as innocuous as *a forum where member states exchange ideas* or as sinister as *a right to bring the policies of member states into line.*

- Article 5: *The Union shall respect the national identities of its member states, inherent in their fundamental structures, political and constitutional, including for regional and local self government. It shall respect their essential state functions, including those for ensuring the territorial integrity of the State, and for maintaining law and order and safeguarding internal security.*

Since a few items, like internal security, territorial integrity have been singled out as worthy of respect, what about other essential state functions, like law, taxation, education, etc. that are not mentioned? Are they less sacrosanct, are they destined to fall eventually within the EU competences?

- Article 11: *The Union shall have competence to co-ordinate the economic and employment policies of the member states. The Union shall have competence to define and implement a common foreign and security policy, including the progressive framing of a common defence policy.*

What kind of co-ordination of employment policies is possible when unemployment levels vary enormously between member states? How can the same policy work both for situations of high unemployment and near full employment? How would the Union have defined a common foreign policy in the lead-up to the war in Iraq? In implementing a common foreign policy, does the Union intend to make the position of a British Foreign Secretary redundant? How does a common defence policy take account of NATO? Which one takes precedence over the other?

- Article 14: *The Union shall adopt measures to ensure co-ordination of the economic policies and employment policies of the member states.*

This is one of the key provisions of the constitution. Note how subtly, with silky smoothness, "co-ordinate" has become "ensure co-ordination". Thus the Union is instructed and empowered to regulate the economic and employment policies of member states. In these vital spheres of people's lives, Westminster is to be no longer the supreme authority.

- Article 15: *Member states shall unreservedly support the Union's common foreign and security policy in a spirit of loyalty and mutual solidarity and shall comply with the Acts adopted by the Union. They shall refrain from action contrary to the Union's interests or likely to impair its effectiveness.*

So if the Union were to decide that a specific form of co-operation between the EU and the US is contrary to the Union's interest, Britain may be obliged to abandon her transatlantic alliance.

- Article 21: *The European Council shall elect its President, by qualified majority, for a term of 2.5 years, renewable once.*

What exactly is this president supposed to do? To be a figurehead or someone wielding substantial power or a fudge between the two? In the measure that he or she is to have decision making responsibilities, someone else is bound to lose them. Who will that be? Heads of the nation states? Brussels Commissioners? The European Parliament? Are we talking here about an eventual *leader* for Europe, or what? Do we really want the voice of an ill-defined European President at the UN, the G8, bilateral and multi-lateral conferences? It is axiomatic that any new centre of authority will strive to accumulate power and influence. Thus a presidency is certain to compete with other existing centres of authority, creating uncertainty, confusion and further divides.

- Article 27: *The European Council, deciding by qualified majority with the agreement of the President of the Commission, shall appoint the Union's Foreign Minister.*

What will be his contribution over and above those of the various national Foreign Ministers? If they all agree among themselves, he is somewhat superfluous. If they do not agree, as over Iraq, he will suffer from an acute form of diplomatic schizophrenia.

- Article 40: *The common security and defence policy shall be an integral part of the common foreign and security policy. It shall provide the Union with an operational capability drawing on assets civil and military.*

A rapid intervention force, employed for humanitarian ends, has long been on the EU agenda. Its establishment, on a small scale, has the backing of the current British government. What is proposed here is of an altogether greater moment: an open-ended requirement for the member states to provide the military means for the implementation of the common foreign and security policy. If this means anything at all, it opens the way to a distinct European military force.

- The entire text of the Charter of Fundamental Rights is to be enshrined in the Constitution. The areas affected by these rights are quite extensive, ranging from strikes, working hours, social security and housing assistance to environmental and consumer protection. As these matters fall mostly within the catch-all basket of shared competences, Union legislation takes precedence. The Westminster Parliament will have to seek permission from The European Court of Justice in Luxemburg to restrict or modify any of them. This charter, of course, does not replace the European Convention of Human Rights, with its court in Strasbourg. The two charters and courts run side by side, overlapping in authority, duplicating tasks, adding further confusion and bureaucracy.

- The Union is to be endowed with a legal personality. Individuals and internationally recognized states have such a status but nobody is quite sure what this means in the European context. This provision may seem academic but it could have serious ramifications in international law. A representative of the Union, such as its future President, may be empowered to sign agreements in the name of the Union, with its terms binding on member states.

- The Union is to be given powers to bring into line criminal laws and penalties as well as to harmonise legal procedures to ensure effective implementation of EU policy. Since this policy affects most areas of daily life, the essential workings of British justice, as it has evolved over the last 900 years, will pass beyond UK control. The draft provides for a European Public Prosecutor with powers to investigate and prosecute within each member state.

Even more significantly, the Constitution introduces profound structural changes to the Union the implications of which go well beyond its individual provisions. The Maastricht Treaty, whatever its shortcomings, established in 1992 a three pillar structure, two of which reserved certain areas of legislature where the nation states enjoyed a clear primacy over the EU. The Constitution brings all previous treaties into a single text, sweeping away the entire pillar structure and the member states' safeguards with it. Those areas, hugely enlarged with significant additions, are now to be found in the melting pot of a newly fabricated category comprising most aspects of human activity: the Internal Market; Freedom, Security, Justice and Foreign Affairs; Agriculture and Fisheries;

Transport; Energy; Social Policy and Social Security; Economic, Social and Territorial Cohesion; Environment; Public Health and Consumer Protection. Entitled *shared competences*, this invention serves multiple purposes. It fudges the distinction between the powers of the Union and member states, it defers the most difficult power transfer issues to episodic future negotiations to take place in a Brussels environment; it paves the way towards a federal Europe without spelling out the program.

One of the principal remits of the Convention was a clear demarcation between the powers of the Union and those of the individual nations. Given the radically divergent objectives of the participants such transparency was unattainable. Instead we have a term that conjures up an image of harmonious collaboration between individual nations and Brussels and is meant to make the whole deal more palatable to those still reluctant to travel the Greater Europe route. In practice, by bequeathing the more painful, detailed decisions to political machinations in a mist-shrouded future, this formulation sets up an enduring tension between the centre and the individual state. It provides a permanent arena for the inevitable power struggle between eccentric and concentric forces. It serves to complicate, confuse and divide the administration of a politically ambiguous continent. It is not without significance that the French equivalent for the term *shared* is *partagée*. The two terms do overlap: the principal use in English is more to do with participation and having things in common, whilst the common French use connotes division. In the most profound sense of *shared competences* and its consequences, the French have it absolutely right.

In one respect at least, the concept of *shared*

competences is unambiguous: this sharing is not between equals. The Union is definitely the senior partner: crucially, only in areas where the union opts not to legislate are member states permitted to do so. This provision gives the game away: there can be no doubt as to primacy. Many of us still remember John Major flaunting subsidiarity after Maastricht like the piece of paper brandished by Chamberlain on his return from Munich. It was supposed to limit the encroachment of EU into the affairs of nation states. The point of subsidiarity was that wherever possible, legislation by national parliaments should take precedence over Union initiatives. Since then, for the last decade, no decision making power has been repatriated under this, or any other, heading. In the proposed constitution the power to enforce the subsidiarity principle is reduced to the status of a suggestion. If a third of the national parliaments request it ...*the Commission shall review its proposal...and may decide to maintain, amend or withdraw it.* No comfort here.

The few attempts in the Convention to reverse this one-way flow of power transfer were smoothly dispatched. Article 95 of the present Treaty allows the Commission to harmonise laws and regulations in the interest of the internal market. As just about anything is being traded across national boundaries the internal market is a very elastic province. The Commission has used Article 95 to generate directives all over the place including money laundering, the art market, metrication, anti-terrorism measures, summer-time adjustments, civil protection, anti-personnel mines and balance of payments support. Although the need to curtail and give a sharper definition to Article 95 was recognised at the working group level, the

Presidium ignored its recommendation, thus leaving the door wide open for the creeping transfer of additional powers to the Union.

A similar fate befell moves to modify Article 308 of the present Treaty ("flexibility clause") that allows the Community, acting unanimously, to assume new powers to achieve treaty objectives. Although it is meant to be applied in the context of common market operations only, it has been employed for such varied purposes as the setting up of new executive agencies and granting loans to non-EU countries. As this flexibility clause is being absorbed into the new Constitution (Article 17), the working group recommended stringent limitations to its scope. Here again the recommendation was ignored, leaving the Union the power to amend the constitution by the backdoor, without going through proper procedures and avoiding the need for ratification by each member state.

In effect, this one way traffic of power transfer is so deeply entrenched in the integrationist agenda that the Constitution contains no mechanism for the review and return of any specific powers from the Union to the member states. No matter how ineffective or counterproductive the Union may prove to be in any given area, there is no way back. The relinquishing of any central power is considered inconceivable.

Perhaps the most glaring absence from the text is any provision to trim back the 97,000 pages of the Euro bible (*acquis communautaire*), to simplify and make more accessible its text and to diminish the unceasing torrent of EU regulations and directives flowing from Brussels, of which 102,567 are now directly applicable to Britain. On the contrary, the upshot of the whole exercise is to extend

Brussels activity, to concentrate decision making powers into an even narrower circle of privileged insiders, to diminish further the role of national parliaments and make government less, not more, democratic. Thus, beyond hugely increasing the Union's sphere of dominance, the Constitution removes the national veto in at least 36 separate policy areas.

What all this means for the man in the street is plain enough. The bulk of the laws affecting his life will be conceived and formulated by an unelected Commission in Brussels, and provided that a majority of Heads of State, representing 60 per cent of the Union's population approve, every one in the land will be subject to them without further ado. Ratification and translation into a law of the land by Parliament will, of course, be a matter of routine. So, for example, if the Commission decides in its wisdom that no one is allowed to work for more than 37 hours a week, and if the Prime Ministers of Spain, Italy, Germany, Poland and those of any combination of nine small countries approve that decision, that's it. From then on anyone caught working longer hours in Britain will be subject to the full rigour of the law, as specified in Brussels. If the Constitution is accepted, such a decision making process would become the British norm.

The government, in the business of selling the Constitution to the British electorate, has been making a great play of the protection afforded by the national veto. The impression Blair and Co take such pains to create is that the veto somehow guarantees British sovereignty, that possessing it eliminates all dangers of European centralization, that exercising it protects the ultimate authority of Westminster. In the first place, the area subject to national vetoes has been gradually shrinking. The Single European Act extended Qualified Majority Voting significantly in 1986; the Maastricht Treaty, with the EMU and the Social Chapter, eroded the veto powers further; the Constitution goes way beyond all that. As an additional refinement, veto protection may be lost permanently in some areas, such as matters relating to energy, social security, planning, water and land management if that is agreed unanimously by the member states.

There is a fundamental flaw in the argument that presents the veto as the ultimate guardian of Britain's independence. In theory, any of the 25 governments could exercise its veto at any time touching any Union decision, within specified limits, that it dislikes. In practice, adherence to unanimity simply does not work. Determined, repeated use of the veto could impair or even paralyse the workings of the EU. Therefore, the 24 other members of the Council will always find a way to neutralize a serious veto. In the case of minor players, say Malta or Latvia, they will be simply bullied into compliance. When one of the major countries threatens to use her veto, Britain at Maastricht being a case in point, we know precisely what political pressures are brought to bear to enforce the centrist will even at the cost of the kind of deeply damaging compromises that have defined the history of the Union. Throughout the long years of the cold war the Soviet Union employed her veto in the Security Council of the UN with great effect. But the Russian *nyet* was an instrument merely to render the UN impotent. In the context of a functioning Union a purely negative use of the veto is not viable. A judicious, highly selective use of the power of veto does provide Britain with a practical tool in the political horse trading that is bound to follow a deadlock. It will not, by itself, stop the Union going her way nor give any nation state a meaningful and permanent exemption from the will of a centrist establishment.

In the latest version of the Constitution, in some parts within the ever shrinking sphere where national vetoes still apply, the exercise of the veto amounts to no more than a temporary suspension of the legislating process to allow for a further review. This weakened version of the veto was termed by its Irish devisers as *an emergency brake*. This is indeed an appropriate name for all forms of veto powers in the EU context. You apply the emergency brake only when the regular means of control are of no avail and the vehicle is about to crash. What the proponents of the Constitution are asking the British public is to buy into a form of transport with superb emergency brakes but lacking the means to control its speed, acceleration, direction or destination. No second hand car dealer would have the nerve to make such an offer, even if it were legal. What is undeniable is that *no government in office is entitled to assert that any particular right of using a veto can furnish even a partial safeguard to British independence.*

We do not know as yet when the referendum on the Constitution is to take place. It is unlikely that the Prime Minister will risk it before the next general election. We do know, however, that throughout the time leading up to it the government's formidable spin resources will be harnessed to present a stark choice facing the British people: in or out of Europe. Even though most of us understand this to be a false dichotomy, the sheer weight of a determined government campaign will suffice to create serious doubt and confusion in the public mind as to what voting on the Constitution is all about. So it is helpful to formulate some simple, relevant questions that can be answered with a degree of certainty.

Does the Constitution transfer additional decision making powers from the member states to the Union? Without doubt, from the current Treaties to the new Constitution the movement is strictly one way. Powers are transferred from nation states to the Union, not the other way around. This is a fact; just how much power is being shifted is a matter of degree, subject to debate.

Is the intent of the Constitution to provide a final definition of EU authority or set guidelines for its future development? Even a very superficial reading of the text leaves one with the clear impression that its architects were less concerned with pinpointing the Union's present parameters than with constructing a road map of a fully integrated political Europe. Both explicitly and implicitly, the language beckons to a future where national divides dwindle into cultural heritages of language and history. Quite clearly, the proposed Constitution is meant to facilitate the transition from an administratively cumbersome present, with something like parity between member states and the Union, to a homogeneous future with Europe more conveniently governed from a single centre of authority.

Does the Constitution help clarify the relationship between the Union and its member states? On the contrary, with almost all difficult issues subject to *shared competence*, with the complex formula of *Qualified Majority Voting*, with regular Vetoes and *Emergency Break Vetoes*, the lines of authority are even more blurred. The future promises more uncertainty, tension, strife and endless political horse trading.

Has the Constitution succeeded in simplifying Union procedures, reducing bureaucracy, creating a freer, more enterprising continent? Not a single provision in the text concerns itself with any of these objectives, so essential for the future of a vibrant Europe. Quite the contrary, the creation of additional institutions, functions and administrative layers, complicates not simplifies the workings of the Union. It increases rather than reduces red tape.

Does the Constitution make the Union more democratic or accountable? At least as these terms are commonly understood in this country, the answer is plainly no. It would have been a surprise to find such a consideration featured at all on any Giscard agenda. The role of the democratically elected national parliaments is diminished and the enlarged powers of the European Parliament are meaningless since less and less people participate in European elections and those taking part vote on national issues and along national party lines. There are simply no Europe-wide political parties with specific agendas to provide a democratic choice for voters in the European parliamentary elections. The people in the streets of Bilbao, Lyons, Gothenburg and Hamburg do not feel that their view makes the slightest difference to what happens in Brussels.

Does the Constitution help unify Europe? This was certainly the stated objective of those who drafted its text. On the face of it, the Union at the centre would become more dominant, more of the decisions affecting people's lives would be taken at Brussels and greater uniformity would prevail across the continent. All this looks fine on paper. Translating the paper into reality, however, would have precisely the opposite effect. As we have seen throughout the brief history of the EU, artificially constructed central directives and Treaty obligations are interpreted with substantial divergence by member states, whilst compliance on the ground has more to do with the individual characteristics of nations than with a theoretical European norm. In fact, the more centralized and political is the decision making process, imposed from the top, the greater will be the variety in local performance and national patterns of actual government. The attempt at artificial conformity to any common denominator merely serves to accentuate the differences in people's real needs, habits and aspirations. The price of a higher European profile is bound to be tension, strife, division and disunity across the continent.

Once the answers to these questions are considered it is difficult to see how anyone in this country could deem the Constitution good for Britain, never mind Europe. People do not have to read the voluminous text or follow the minutiae of the arguments, to understand instinctively that it threatens to erode their nationhood. They are not willing to give any more power to Brussels, they are tired of unending treaties, directives and regulations emanating from Europe, they want nothing to do with a grandiloquent document written by continental politicians in a concentric tradition. Just as they did not need Gordon Brown's tests to have instinctively understood the meaning of joining the Euro. The British electorate is savvy enough to understand the broad outlines and judge the main implications of the constitution. Blair and Co, through its serial focus groups and continuous internal polling, are well aware that a referendum cannot be won on the merits of the case. This is why their argument will center not on the provisions of the Constitution itself but on the terrible fate awaiting Britain if she dared to reject it. Their hope is that the debate will be twisted into one between pro and anti Europeans and divide the electorate along party lines with the general public confused by semantic detail and bored out of its mind.

We had a sample of this kind of government spin during the European elections in May this year. On the various TV channels, right through a night of post-mortem analysis we heard the Chairman of New Labour and a selection of cabinet ministers, Peter Hain, Charles Clarke and Patricia Hewitt among them, repeat, as some sort of mantra, the nonsensical formula that Europe means 3 million UK jobs. To every reasoned argument the endlessly reiterated uniform response was simply "Europe = 3 million jobs". Someone, somewhere must have convinced the Labour leadership that the Goebbels formula really works: *tell a blatant lie consistently and often enough and people will come to believe it.* Maybe in Nazi Germany but not in 21st-century Britain. Especially when a lie is as primitive as this. Everyone knows that the continent's trade balance with Britain is positive, that Britain is the most important market for continental goods. Everyone knows that EU regulations and the introduction of the Euro have contributed to the high rates of unemployment in the major European economies. Everyone knows that jobs have been so successfully created here by a relatively benign tax regime, by tolerant and tolerable labour laws, by relative ease of doing business, by massive inward investment and by the enterprise of the people. And everyone also knows that rejecting the Constitution will make no difference to any of these underlying facts.

Still, the question of what happens to Britain after a no vote in a referendum is an interesting one. On the continent, the rejection of this Constitution by the British electorate would make a substantial difference, not necessarily the way the government would like us believe. Even if Britain were the only state not to ratify the Constitution, she would not be expelled from the EU. It is just hypothetically possible that the other 24 states would formally agree to disband the Union and inaugurate a new one founded on the Constitution but this seems very unlikely. If the requirement of unanimity means what it says and if the power of veto has any meaning at all, the proposed Constitution would be taken off the agenda altogether or it would be back to the drawing board for something less ambitious, more practical, more user-friendly. In either case the Union would continue to function in the interim just as well or as badly as before. The only noticeable difference would be a slight, but welcome, diminution in the flow of EU legislation and Brussels directives.

Many integrationists, at home and abroad, would undoubtedly rail against the eccentric British and paint a dire future for an isolated, marginalized, politically emasculated island on the edge of a flourishing, harmonious and united continent. But this is just rhetoric, and not very convincing rhetoric at that. The very same warnings about Britain outside the Euro turned out to be empty threats. For those politicians and statesmen on the continent who still believe in the future of nation states and for the vast majority of European individuals, this single act in defiance of a seemingly unstoppable trend, would take Britain to the very heart of the continent. This act of true leadership, against centralisation, against the erosion of native democracies, against a vast, amorphous state-in-becoming, would serve to encourage other nations, other political forces, other independent thinkers to follow suit. It would demonstrate that it is possible to reverse the fashionable flow, to reduce dreams of a political Union to the viable reality of a Union whose fundamentals, as its origins, are economic.

To reject a badly drafted constitution is important enough. But, perhaps, even more so are the lessons to be learnt from the entire constitutional exercise for it serves to demonstrate the gulf between British and concentric political cultures. On the continent, especially in France and Germany, political initiatives tend to originate from the top, devised by a closely knit establishment whose members, even though they may often be in opposition, form an elite group. Over at least the last three hundred years significant political change in Britain has come about as a result of organised pressure from the grass roots. The chief agents of change have mostly been back benchers in parliament, public opinion, the media, non-conformist movements or exceptional individuals outside the ambit of professional politics. All major political innovation on the continent, like the drafting of this Constitution, proceeds in the first place from a conceptual template, into which subsequent reality has somehow to fit. In Britain it proceeds from changing realities that evolve their own implicit conceptual framework.

The continuous consent of the governed is not, generally speaking, a continental requirement. Consulting the public is a nominal exercise, well exemplified by the activities of this Convention. The publishing of green papers and white papers preceding any legislation, public debates through the media, the letter column of *The Times*, the formation of spontaneous pressure groups, like CND, the anti-poll tax brigade or the Countryside Alliance, are peculiarly British phenomena. A continental politician, worthy of the name, must have a grand vision. A political document of any importance must be impregnated with noble sentiment and set forth ideals that can never be attained. At Westminster, politicians struggle to conjure up even a modest vision and political parties try hard to make specific promises which, of course, they are almost never quite able to keep. Somehow or other, irrespective of the starting point, the outcome of continental legislation tends to reinforce central authority whilst its British counterpart had, until recently, the opposite effect.

One other lesson that British politicians regularly fail to heed is that they have no hope of outplaying the French in the art of diplomacy. Once they agreed to have a written constitution, once they consented to have Giscard d'Estaing as head of the Convention, with the Brussels club and the European parliament given major roles, the outcome could never have been in doubt: a document so rich in ambiguities, so opaque, inviting so many interpretations, so abstract, so quintessentially continental, so perfectly designed to drown all resistance in a gluey sea of pure semantics. Admittedly, the choice of Peter Hain to represent British interests was not exactly inspired. Lacking a European background, inexperienced in continental negotiations, shifting his principles from complete rejection of British participation in the Union to its total embrace, the British Minister for Europe proved feeble, naive and highly amenable. Not that any other member of a Blair cabinet would have made a crucial difference.

This referendum presents a great opportunity. Britain is admirably placed to take up the challenge and save Europe once more from the worst excesses of her own ideologies. The proposed Constitution has nothing to do with the people of Europe. They have not sought it and have not been consulted in the making of it. It is a compilation of words by politicians for politicians to the exclusion of all practicality and common sense. The process of its creation and implementation will have served to divide the people of Europe rather than unite them. If implemented, the damage would not just be to the integrity of nation states, but also to the long-term future of the Union itself. The premature forcing of a complex strait jacket on what is still a young and evolving organisation would inevitably delay the natural coming together of the diverse European nations. For those who wish to see Britain closer to Europe, this constitutional exercise is something of a disaster.

A constitution is only as good as the democratic culture in which it is rooted. As de Tocqueville, a great student of constitutional law, once observed, its success depends on "the manners and customs" of the people. That of the US endures; the Weimar one is long forgotten. If and when Europe succeeds in welding herself into a single cohesive democracy, she may devise a reasonably written constitution. By then she would not need one.

13

The Euro

...The history of Europe is littered with examples of monetary unions that had promising starts but subsequently collapsed. On present form, Emu may be heading in the direction as some of its ill-fated predecessors of the late 19th and early 20th-centuries. Their failure was ultimately due to a lack of political integration...
Wolfgang Munchau,
the *Financial Times*, September 6th 2004

The government has stated its clear intention to take Britain into the Euro zone when economic conditions are "right". The country is promised a referendum on the subject but we do not know its date, its exact wording or the terms of the debate set by the government to support taking such a radical step. It is even possible that far-reaching future amendments to the European Constitution will make the adoption of a single currency mandatory on member states and thus obviate the need for a separate decision. As New Labour came to power, the switch of currencies was presented as a mere technical matter, conducive to easier trade and travel, without constitutional or far-reaching economic implications and therefore without the need to consult the people. Broad opposition to the Euro forced the government to shift its ground. Its effect on the economy of the country became central to the issue and Gordon Brown's five "objective" tests appeared on the horizon. Now, with the admission that economic tests are never likely to be clear and unambiguous, the political dimension of the coming decision cannot be easily disguised.

Currencies

It may be helpful to discuss briefly, at the risk of stating the obvious, the basic function of any currency. Does it matter who has the authority to mint coins, print notes, control and regulate the state's financial instruments, borrow and lend funds, set interest rates, etc.? What difference does it make if we swap the Bank of England for the European Central Bank in Frankfurt?

The most obvious use of a currency is as a means of trading. A hard currency is one that facilitates trading. A soft currency makes trading difficult. The US Dollar, the Swiss Franc, the Deutschemark, the Yen are prime examples of the former whilst the Greek Drachma, the Polish Zloty and the many assorted African moneys are used in international trade only as a last resort. Sterling, always considered a hard currency, had a somewhat chequered career after the war before achieving a respectable level of stability and strength over the last twelve years.

Generally speaking, independent states have always insisted on having their own currency. The aim, with varying degrees of success, has been the maintaining of its value. One cannot easily find a historic example of a state renouncing its own currency whilst maintaining its independence. Even within the Zollverein, a powerful and long enduring customs union at the centre of Europe, each member state retained her own currency until they were all officially incorporated into the German Empire in the 19th-century. The US Dollar came into being after, not before, the creation of the United States. Why has it been considered so universally important to have one's own kind of money?

There is, of course, an element of national or dynastic pride. One of the first acts of every newly crowned sovereign in history was to have coins minted in his and her likeness to advertise and further legitimise the new authority. After the comprehensive defeat of Germany in the Second World War, with a divided country governed by a constitution imposed by their conquerors and forbidden armed forces, the Deutschemark was the single most cherished icon to help restore German self-respect. As it increased in strength and importance, surpassing even the currencies of some of the victors, so grew German self-confidence, sense of identity, national unity and economic purpose. Every time a German tourist went abroad, every time a German company imported goods, a deep sense of satisfaction accompanied the transaction, a warm glow illuminated the German heart.

Thus owning one's currency is not just a matter of pride, it is also a focal point of national identity. It is part of what unites and binds people into the state of which they are citizens. Carrying the same notes in our wallets as our fellows and trading them with each other by using the same notes makes us also, in part, the same people. The state of the currency also acts as a barometer of the country's economic health. Its value, in terms of other currencies, signals the weakness or the strength of the economic life that sustains it. For nothing demonstrates better the true value of your economy than the confidence of the potential buyers of your currency. Without having this external measure it is not so easy to assess clearly how well the country, as a whole, is performing.

A currency is founded on a financial institution that designs and controls its coins and notes, guarantees its legitimacy, and is responsible for protecting its intrinsic value. In the case of Sterling these are the principal roles of the Bank of England. Before World War One, the Governor of the Bank of England promised to pay 1 gold sovereign for each and every £1 bank note submitted to him. Having abandoned the gold standard, for many decades of the last century central banks were supposed to protect the value of their currencies by controlling the quantity of bank notes in circulation and the debt notes they issued in their own denomination. These amounts were supposed to bear a close relationship to the banks' reserves, gold or otherwise, and the nation's ability to repay these debts in a timely fashion. Thus, if the issue of bank notes and debit notes were excessive, the value of the currency would diminish, akin to the physical debasing of the coinage by Henry VIII.

With the increasing complexity and sophistication of financial transactions, depending less and less on actual bank notes, the central banks' means of protecting currency value is now confined to manipulation of debt and, above all, control of inflation. After all, the value of a currency may also be expressed in terms of its purchasing power. Of course, the incurring of public debt and the management of inflation are to some degree in the hands of the government but the central banks' influence in major western economies over the second half of the 20th-century has been crucial. It is impossible to envisage the rise of Germany as an economic giant in the absence of the Bundesbank, or the flourishing of the US in the last decade without reference to the Federal Reserve Board. It is not the fact that Alan Greenspan sets the interest rates, it is not that he controls the timing and terms of issuing treasury notes, important as these powers are. It is the profound influence he wields over the President and Congress and the confidence he inspires in financial markets, that has such a bearing on the value of the US Dollar. The same could be said about the successive Presidents of the Bundesbank from the fifties onwards.

The Bank of England, in the corresponding periods, did not attain the same status and has wielded its powers to a lesser extent. Currently, with its newly acquired independence the Bank's authority is growing steadily again. In any case, the principle remains the same: a national currency, governed by a national bank, is an integral part of the management of the country's economy. This impacts on financial reserves, taxation policies, borrowings, ability to attract inward investment and the capacity to trade successfully both within the country's own market and throughout the world. So the issue is not just one of giving up the right to mint coins, print notes or set interest rates. It is losing independence on fiscal policy, and therefore, on public spending, on how much or how little is spent, for example on the National Health Service. What the British people have to decide on entering the Euro zone, is whether to give up effective control of the economic life of the country.

Origin and Objective

What made the Euro happen? Was it, for example, the outcome of irresistible pressure exercised by the unified forces of Big Business, industrial giants and commercial interests? It is certainly true that the fluctuating values of different currencies add to the complexities of international trading, financial transactions and industrial investment decisions. Buying and selling patterns with international partners are smoother in one and the same currency. Yet Sir Christopher Gent, the recent chairman of Vodafone and a leading advocate of Euro membership, reported that "Movements in exchange rates had no material impact on the total group operating profit...in any of the three years ended March 31st, 2003." The greatest part of Britains trade, 60%, is denominated in Dollars, therefore it is not surprising that, based on 2001 figures, the cost to hedge sterling against the euro is calculated to cost the UK about 0.05 per cent of GDP, not a significant factor in any equation. Still, on the face of it, any multinational company or any business involved in exports and imports should benefit from currency simplification. Nevertheless, business communities throughout the continent by no means universally supported the Euro project. In Germany, for example, a great many leaders of industry voiced severe reservations that are intensifying day by day. In Britain, we know that the CBI, the Institute of Directors and various associations representing smaller companies, are all divided on the subject, with increasing majorities against adopting the Euro. The same is true elsewhere.

For business the Euro is something less than an unmixed blessing. The drawbacks of trading in diverse currencies have been part of international commerce from time immemorial. The Euro will not eliminate them. For the foreseeable future, Euro countries will still have to buy almost all their oil in dollars. Key components for their industries from Japan, Korea, China and the US will still be traded in dollars as will the vast array of consumer goods imported from overseas. The fluctuations in the relative values of the dollar and the Euro will be of greater consequence than any changes in the relative value of European national currencies have ever been. Within my own industry sector, toys and games, so heavily dependent on Chinese manufacture, there have already been a significant number of bankruptcies due to the rapid decline of the Euro against the Dollar. The vital difference is that from now on the business community in any country within the Euro zone will exercise much less influence on its own currency than it ever did before.

If it had been merely a technical matter of easing trade and investment within Europe a common currency could easily have been created without recourse to the drastic step of eliminating national currencies. Indeed such a pre-Euro currency, the Ecu, did come into being and was employed in banking circles for some years. Its basis was a weighted basket of European currencies (Mark, Franc, Guilder, Sterling, etc). Thus, any Ecu transaction involving European countries largely obviated currency risk exposure, the value being determined by a sort of European average. In terms of practical convenience, this is in effect what the Euro is doing. Of course, the Ecu was a modest affair. It was not meant to replace the national currencies and it was not backed by a European central bank that usurped the role of the national ones. It required no loss of national independence in financial, economic and political domains.

The chances are that had it been allowed to develop organically, its use encouraged by the national banks, the Ecu would have gained wider and wider acceptance in international trade. As it gained in popularity the national banks could have given it greater legitimacy by gradually increasing the proportion of Ecu-denominated bonds. Later on, Ecu coins and paper notes would have made their appearance in the hands of the general public. As a floating currency its value would have fluctuated in relation to the Dollar and also, to a much lesser extent, in relation to each individual European currency. To the extent that national economies converged with the European median, their currencies would have tracked the Ecu. The responsibility of maintaining the value of any individual currency would have been left to each respective government. Having no fixed exchange rates, currency speculation would not have been an issue. Running side by side with existing national currencies, the Ecu's ultimate fate would have been decided by a population of a few hundred millions of people actually using it. If they preferred the new currency to the old ones, the national currencies would have withered away, leading to a single European common currency. This currency would have been quite a different one to the Euro. Having come into being as a result of a practical need, fulfilling a demand created by altered trading patterns, legitimised by popular endorsement in the real markets, it would have had the strength, the stability derived from its proven track record.

Such a process is one of gradual evolution, nourished by the willing participation of the people, meeting rather than creating market demand, legitimising existing practice, not one of imposing laws and regulations from above in anticipation of an untried and untested future reality. In other words, a typically British phenomenon. But this is not the way things are done on the continent. Driven centrally from above by a committed political establishment, the Euro was presented as one of the most significant milestones on the road to the realisation of a Greater Europe. Appropriate fanfare accompanied every announcement of its laboured progress from conception to realisation. A variety of deadlines were set, huge pressures applied, intensive last-minute negotiations conducted into the small hours of the morning to heighten the dramatic effect and raise the profile of a glamorous new symbol of European unity.

It was not business, as a cohesive, unified force across the continent, that wished to accomplish, or could ever have accomplished the demise of 12 national currencies. But if not business, what else drove the Euro? Was it the Bundesbank and the French National Bank who felt a sudden collective urge to shed their power and resign their responsibilities? All the evidence points to the contrary. Mitterrand had a hard time in bringing the high officials of an august national institution into line and the President of the Bundesbank at the critical moment made his deep concerns as public as German political traditions permit. They, like the then Governor of the Bank of England, Eddie George, felt distinctly uneasy about abandoning control of their own currency.

If neither demanded by business, nor encouraged by the financial institutions of the various nations, did the Euro rise on the waves of an overwhelming popular demand? Did the German people feel bored with their treasured Mark and feel a sudden urge to ditch it? Did the French populace rise and demonstrate against the admittedly dodgy Franc? Quite the contrary. It took Mitterrand a massive publicity campaign, employing the full resources of the centralised government machine, to secure a wafer-thin majority in favour of endorsing the Maastricht Treaty, which set up the Economic and Monetary Union. The referendum, with the Euro question masked by other topics, was timed, administered and conducted by a totally committed central government. As for the Germans, Helmut Kohl did not specifically consult the people on a matter of vital importance to them, but then German political tradition encourages the leader to make those kind of decisions himself. Even so, the German Chancellor felt obliged to justify sacrificing the Mark by two extraordinary and incredible claims. The first guaranteed a Euro that would *at the very least* be as stable as the Mark. The second guaranteed that the adoption of the Euro would make it impossible for wars ever to be fought between European nations.

If anyone suggested taking a wine with a fine pedigree, bearing the label of a famous Chateau, produced from grapes of a great vintage, and then diluting it with younger, cruder, cheaper wines in order to obtain a blend with three or four times the volume and at least as good a quality, such a suggestion would be treated either as a joke or an invitation to commit fraud. Amazingly, this precise proposition was swallowed in Germany and was taken seriously even beyond her borders.

The second claim is even more mystifying. What wars could Kohl have had in mind? Not presumably one between Greece and Denmark, or Portugal and Holland, or Italy and Spain, or Britain and France. The only meaningful reference must have been to Germany herself, one of the principal authors of three European wars in this period, all of them leading to the partial or entire occupation of France. So the Kohl message, to make any sense, must read something like this: the Euro is essential in preventing Germany, the dominant continental power, from starting any territorial wars against her neighbours. Even stated thus the claim is unsustainable but the message conveyed to the German people is that it is worthwhile sacrificing the Mark on the altar of a Europe peacefully embraced by an economically dominant Germany. A common currency in itself is no guarantee against wars. Maybe Kohl, was thinking not of a common currency but of a common economy and some sort of federal state. But this weakens his argument even further, for the most vicious, enduring, hopeless wars are fought by people of different ethnic origins, race, religion, class and ideologies sharing the same economy, territory and state. One need not look any further than the Europe of the 20th-century: Spain, Ireland, the Balkans and Russia, for example, not to mention the American Civil War the century before.

So if the Euro was not the child of a spontaneous popular demand for a unified European currency, whose infant is it? No mystery here. In line with all post war political developments on the continent, the Euro was the product of a Franco-German deal, embodied in this instance by François Mitterrand and Helmut Kohl and manfully supported by the ruling political establishment of both countries. The project was pursued and directed by an increasingly powerful Brussels apparatus headed by the able and committed French Socialist leader, Jacques Delors.

The Franco-German axis has been at the heart of an emerging Western Europe since the early sixties. Both nations, we must not forget, were defeated, occupied and humiliated in World War Two. Both nations faced a dangerous Communist foe, Germany with over a third of its territory still occupied and France with a Marxist party supported by over a third of the electorate and a majority of the all-powerful unions. The new alliance of these traditional rivals, although complex, rested on a simple premise: France was to be given the principal political role in the shaping of a post-war Europe, a Europe with Germany as its economic core. The Franco-German deal, that formed the basis of the original Common Market (the Rome Treaty), as customary with European Treaties, heavily favoured the French in virtually every sphere. Not only did it give them a decisive say in the establishment of administrative functions, in the formulation of rules and regulations, in setting the political style, but it also went a long way in protecting French agriculture, trade, industry, state-owned manufacture and services. In addition Germany agreed to pay a yearly subsidy to France by being a net contributor to the Common Market funds whilst France, as usual, remained a beneficiary. This subsidy, although annually smaller than the reparations paid by Germany in the wake of World War One, already exceeds them in total and appears to be of an indefinite duration.

Despite these built-in advantages, designed to maintain

some sort of parity between the allies, the economic performance of the two nations continued to diverge. Measured by whatever scale, growth of GDP, rate of inflation, government debt, productivity, labour relations, investment, value of currency, the contrast could not have been starker. Whilst France lurched from one economic crisis to another, effectively devaluing its currency with monotonous regularity, the German economy grew from strength to strength, its performance faultless, its currency, the Deutschemark, a model of stability. This divergence, clear for all to behold, became a formidable obstacle to French political ambitions of setting the European agenda. To overcome this obstacle, to bring the economies of the two countries into some sort of alignment, a drastic measure had to be taken. This measure is in effect the Euro.

The idea of a single currency had long been part of the Brussels blueprint for European integration, but it did not come truly alive until the fall of the Berlin Wall in 1989. We now know for a fact that Mitterrand's support of Kohl's historic mission to unify Germany was conditional on the abolition of the Deutschemark. For the French political establishment, the attractions of the Euro are easy to see. The endemic weakness of the Franc has always been a handicap to French political pretensions. Its feeble performance against a virile Mark was a constant reminder of a serious handicap. By merging the currencies this embarrassment would be removed, while it was hoped the excellence of the Mark would rub off on the Euro. With the financial disciplines of the Bundesbank transferred to a new European Central Bank and imposed on French economic management, France would perhaps be able to emulate Germany and somehow keep up with her. In addition,

France would gain a stronger say over monetary policy than she had when at the mercy of the Bundesbank. Although built on the solid foundations of the Mark, and located in Frankfurt, this new financial centre, as originally agreed between the partners, would have been under French management with a French President at least for the first 8 years of its life, had it not been for the fact that France's favoured candidate was mired in fraud allegations. The election of the Dutch Wim Duisenberg as the first President of the ECB was regarded as a temporary setback, to be remedied later.

From a German perspective, the attractions of the Euro were by no means obvious. By the late eighties the Mark had become one of the leading currencies in the world. It certainly set the European benchmark with the Swiss Franc and the Dutch Guilder, among others, tracking it over a long period of time. Bonds denominated in Marks were highly respected by the financial community, ensuring a constant flow of funds. Thus the German government could always borrow money relatively cheaply and keep its long-term debt well under control. More significantly, the gradually appreciating value of the Mark had no negative effect on the competitive edge of German industry. Exports, the driving force of the economy, rose in line with the rising Mark. Indeed, the growing economic influence of Germany within Europe, particularly in the central and eastern regions of the continent, could have made the Mark eventually the preferred currency of the EU, *de facto*, if not *de jure*.

There being no economic need to abolish the cherished Mark, why did Germany embark on the Euro adventure? The only possible reason is one of a specific political agenda, sustained by personal ambition. The objective of the Franco-German alliance could not be realised without deeper economic and political integration of the European states. The forces that drove the Euro have always openly acknowledged it to be a vital component of such a process, an essential means to maintain the centralising momentum. German unification, and expected German economic dominance, was more easily accommodated, more comfortably perceived in an integrated European context. The German people, quite rightly given recent history, were sensitive to the hostility that such dominance generates. They did not wish to be *seen* as too powerful and the sacrifice of the Mark certainly helped.

Even so, getting rid of the Mark was not so easily accomplished. The original deal between France and Germany provided precise and specific assurances that the new currency would live, in all respects, by the highest standards set by the Mark. There was to be a strict adherence to conditions relating to inflation, national debt, pre-entry stability of the individual currencies, national balance sheets, etc. The idea was to restrict entry into the Euro to Germany, France and, for the sake of appearances, the Netherlands and Luxembourg. Unfortunately, the French could not adhere to the terms of the deal: they could not deliver.

At this point in Euro history, had economic considerations been accorded primacy, the project would have been postponed. What mattered, however, was the political agenda and so the economic and financial goalposts were not so much moved as increased to the size of half the pitch. The trouble with that neat manoeuvre was that now not only France could ease herself into the Euro, so could just about every country in the EU. There was a half-hearted attempt to phase the entry of rank outsiders like the Italian Lira but in the end all those currencies that wished to join, with the exception of the Greek Drachma, could do so from the very beginning. The shenanigans involved in the Euro's emergence are too familiar to need reciting. No one will forget the shambles of the ERM or the unseemly haggle over the appointment of the first head of the European Central Bank. The French, having achieved every one of their objectives, were outraged at not having their own promised president safely installed. A desperate urgency was infused into the later stages of the process with the Franc, despite a German lifeline, barely clinging to the ERM and Helmut Kohl's career nearing its scandal ridden end. European leaders went to extreme lengths: suitcases full of French government money were spirited across the Swiss border into German party coffers to help sustain Kohl in power.

In driving the Euro project, the role of Jacques Delors should never be forgotten. It was at least the equal of Mitterrand's and Kohl's. The official line has always been that the European Commission is *merely* a sort of civil service there to implement political decisions reached at Inter-Governmental level. This may be the theory, it certainly is not the practice. Stalin was *merely* the secretary of a Politburo headed by Lenin and we all know what happened to Trotsky, Bucharin and the rest of its heavyweight members. The parish clerk, the planning officer of a county council, the senior civil servant of any ministry, will always exercise a disproportionate degree of power. They have greater knowledge and are more intimately involved with day-to-day decisions than their masters. Accumulation and exercise of power is their stock-in-trade.

Throughout his tenure Delors ensured that European political integration in general, and the Euro in particular, were to be the focus and guiding principle of the Brussels apparatus. All communications emanating from the commission, whether verbal or written, all statistical data, all "expert" opinion, all policy recommendations bore the clear hallmark of an obsessive pre-occupation with the economic and political union of Europe of which the Euro was one of the principal pillars. For the more closely Europe is united, the greater is the power of Brussels and the more illustrious the stature of its leaders. In sum, the prime objective of the Euro was to provide the glue to hold the European Union together. If it does not work out, however, this glue may well bring the Union to a sticky end.

Status and Future Prospects

The Euro is now a tangible reality. Its coins and notes have replaced those of the Deutschemark, the French Franc, the Italian Lira and the other nine now defunct national currencies. Travellers, tourists and holidaymakers are spared the excessive and irritating costs of changing small amounts of money whenever they cross a border. Business communities across the Euro zone are free from the burden and expense of translating currency values for internal transactions. The shoppers are getting used to thinking in Euros and are learning to give up comparing the cost of a purchase to its equivalent in a previous currency. Once the novelty wears off, the popular perception of the Euro will be that of a regular currency, like the Dollar or the Yen.

This, of course, is not the case. The Euro is a highly

unusual currency, a currency like no other. Its coins and notes are not the authorised monetary units of any one sovereign state. The central bank that guarantees its legitimacy and is responsible for protecting its value comes under the jurisdiction of no single country. The bank's reserves, essential to the day-to-day management of the currency, are not fully within its own physical control. The appointment of the bank's president is not in the hands of an elected, legitimate government. The Euro is not grounded in the economy of any one single state. In fact, the Euro of today is a political construct and thus an artificial currency.

Being an artificial currency has far reaching implications. The value of a regular currency, as determined by an open market, reflects the strength of the economy that sustains it, the credibility of the central national bank and the political stability of the nation that owns it. Financial markets take all these considerations into account when trading the currency. In the case of the Euro, it is not one economy but twelve separate economies that have to be evaluated, economies with different strengths and weaknesses, with significant variations of growth and inflation. The credibility of the infant European Central Bank is, as yet, far from secure. Neither Wim Duisenberg nor Jean Claude Trichet is an Alan Greenspan and the governing body of twelve independent national delegates has but a fraction of the authority of the FED. Most important of all, the Euro is subject not only to the degree of political stability *within* each of the twelve constituent states but also to the harmony, cohesiveness and smooth progressive integration of an emerging Greater Europe. This means that the upheavals of every summit, every row over annual contributions of member states, every decision limiting national sovereignty, every political crisis, every decision as to the pace and final form of integration has, and will continue to have, a vital bearing on the stability of the single European currency.

Is it any surprise therefore that the Euro has been so excessively volatile? For the first three years of its existence it lost not only over 20 per cent of its value against the Dollar but also suffered in relation to Sterling, the Yen and the Swiss Franc. Over the following year its value increased sharply against other currencies despite the poor performance of the Euro zone economies. This rise poses new and unexpected threats to exports, extinguishing any hopes of a fast recovery from what is effectively a stagnant situation. Worse still, the European Central Bank cannot radically lower interest rates whilst establishing the credibility of this infant, fragile currency. This is not what the architects of the Euro expected, it is not what they promised to the European peoples.

To realise the political vulnerability of the Euro one has only to imagine a scenario where Alan Greenspan, and members of the FED governing board, are not appointed by, and not answerable to, the President but a motley collection of politicians from Texas to Ohio, each representing local interests and fighting their particular corner. One may also ask what would have happened to the Mark without the close relationship between the Chancellor and the President of the Bundesbank at critical junctures of the German economic renaissance?

Inflation in Ireland has been creeping up to disconcerting levels, way beyond what is permitted by the Euro rules. The Irish government has no viable means of remedying the situation, other than taxation, since interest rates are set in Frankfurt and they are heading down. But even the lever of taxation may be lost by moves towards tax "harmonisation" across the EU. As Ireland, with its 3 million population, is a very minor factor in the European equation, her troubles are easily dismissed. But one has to wonder what will happen when the economic interests of one or two of the major economies run counter to those of the majority? If, for example, German and French economic patterns were seriously to diverge, how would a French or German president of the ECB react then? How would such a clear case of conflict of interest be resolved? How would those who lost out in such a resolution accept the decision? In the course of a prolonged world recession will the industries of all the countries in Europe suffer to the same degree? Or will the stronger ones survive better than the weaker ones? How will the resulting tensions within the Euro and the ECB affect Europe's ability to cope with a crisis of some magnitude?

Such questions trouble only those who have reservations about the future course of European integration. Those committed to a unified Europe believe that serious economic divergence within Europe is simply no longer possible. And what guarantees this future harmony is, of course, the Euro itself. Here then is the crux of the whole argument. It is now generally admitted that the *present* state of the Euro is not very healthy. It is unpopular with large segments of the German public even though they are resigned to it, whilst the Danes, the Swedes and British show no enthusiasm to fall into its ambitious embrace. But for the architects of the Euro its current volatility is of little concern. For them the Euro of today is merely a temporary device, a transitional stage leading to a currency of an altogether different dimension: a Euro that is the unquestioned financial instrument of a fully integrated Greater Europe. As the ERM was a necessary step towards the Euro, so the current Euro is a necessary step on the way to the ultimate European currency. So when discussing the longer term future prospects of the Euro, a clear distinction has to be drawn between the Euro as we know it today and the currency of a politically united Europe.

The current Euro, with its anomalous position, untried and untested, subject to twelve different political masters, less stable than its creators promised, has a dubious future. Some would say no future at all. For the first time, the German bank WestLB is openly speculating whether the Euro will survive beyond the next five to eight years while Jean Claude Trichet, the new president of the ECB, defined his prime objective over the next few years as the building of confidence in the currency. He has his work cut out. The Growth and Stability Pact, forged in 1996 to underpin the Euro, is now in tatters. The European Court of Justice condemned the EU finance ministers for shelving the Pact but allowed France and Germany to escape the disciplinary measures consequent on blatantly breaching its rules. This means the European Central Bank is bound to become even more reluctant to ease monetary policy, leaving the Eurozone a stagnant island in a booming global economy for years to come. At the same time, all national governments have now an open license to ignore the Pact's 3 per cent deficit limit with its attendant sanctions. On cue, Italy has just adopted a new budgetary plan that is expected to increase its deficit for 2005 to around 5 per cent of GDP. Not surprisingly Italy's credit rating has been degraded by Standard & Poor's.

A government that has no responsibility for the value of its currency nor for the level of interest rates has no incentive to limit its borrowing. Quite the reverse, it has every incentive to borrow as much as it can get away with, taking full advantage of the fiscal restraint of other members of the same currency zone. This is precisely why the Stability Pact was devised in the first place. Paradoxically, in the eurozone every government is now effectively borrowing in a foreign currency, over which it has no control. Thus Italy is now more susceptible to going bankrupt than it ever was with its own weak Lira. Her debt downgrade is the first sign that the financial markets have taken on board the fundamental flaw at the core of the Euro.

Significant as these first cracks in the fabric of the Euro may be, far more serious dangers to its longevity are posed by what is happening in Germany. Over the last two or three years, since the effective loss of the Mark, the German economy has suffered not just in relation to major world economies but also, most significantly, measured against those of her Euro zone partners. The financial burdens of absorbing the defunct economy of East Germany, the heavy contributions to Brussels, and the restrictive framework of the Euro, have created a very uneven playing field. Rules and regulations affecting the economy are more rigorous and more rigorously enforced in Germany than elsewhere in the eurozone, the tax regime is more severe, and there is no longer a compensating advantage of a strong and stable currency. It is hardly surprising therefore that industrialists now prefer to locate their operations in countries like Portugal or Ireland, being exposed to no currency risks and having the best of both worlds. We cannot tell just for how long the German public will put up with the decline of their country merely to assuage a collective, and diminishing, sense of guilt about the Second World War.

Financial analysts have already begun actively to plot the implications of a disintegrating Euro. For a start, that could mean higher bond yields, wider spreads between countries and a steeper yield curve. Then, the demise of the Euro as a significant reserve currency. Further down the road, in certain circumstances Germany could decide to leave the Euro, introducing a New Deutschemark as a more stable and stronger currency. Existing cross-border transactions would be honoured in euros to the advantage of the higher-valued Deutschemark. It is thought that the practical and technical hurdles to the break-up of the Euro are much lower than has been generally presumed. The national central banks are still fully operational, conducting the regular open-market operations to provide liquidity on a national basis. Hence, they are fully equipped to operate a national monetary policy from day one. More significantly, the bulk of the reserves are still held by the national central banks. Even the euro notes and coins are country specific. For the coins, the flipside carries a national design. For the banknotes, the letter before the serial number indicates the issuing national central bank. Thus a country could simply decide to use its own euro notes and coins as legal tender until new coins are minted and notes are printed to embody the national currency.

The Euro of a united Europe is quite another matter. As a conventional currency, like the Dollar, Yen or Rouble, its future prospects will mirror, grosso modo, the economic prosperity of the state it serves. In a coherent European federation the value of its currency would rise and fall with its economic performance. In this sense the creators of the Euro and its backers are right. In fairness to them they never seriously tried to disguise the underlying political agenda. This agenda of closer and closer European integration is not only freely discussed on the continent, it is continually taking place. Every European summit over the last three decades has resulted in the transfer of powers to Brussels. It is a one-way traffic. The heated midnight debates of the leaders concern only the speed of political integration; its desirability has seldom been in question.

Since we cannot envisage with any degree of certainty the course of European integration, predicting the future prospect of the Euro, with or without British participation, would be a hazardous enterprise. For all we know, it may one day in the distant future rival, or even surpass the mighty Dollar, as its more ambitious backers hope. On the other hand, it may struggle and languish at the bottom end of the international currency tables for years to come. It is not improbable that the Euro will disappear altogether, as currencies of better pedigree have in the past after major political or economic realignments.

14

The Chancellor's Five Tests

*Examinations are formidable even to the best
prepared, for the greatest fool may ask
more than the wisest man can answer*
Charles Caleb Colton
Lacon

Since it is now generally accepted that the five tests cannot
yield a sufficiently clear and unambiguous result to justify
British entry, some people may regard this chapter as
superfluous. However, as no one can foretell the statistics
that will issue from the Treasury, nor the spin a government
determined to join the Euro may put on them, the criteria
are worth a brief consideration. The list of five tests - the
City, employment, inward investment, flexibility and
convergence - is rather reminiscent of laundry lists agonised
over by some people about to commit to a lifelong
relationship. These itemise such human qualities as
warmth, loyalty, brains, sense of humour, strength of
character, selfishness, earning power, capacity to love,
independence, etc. Now both these lists have a great deal in
common:

- They are supposed to help in forming an objective judgment.
- The number of items on the list is pretty arbitrary, could be 3,5,9 or whatever.
- The items listed are supposed to be independent of each other.
- The decision is often made already and the scoring is adjusted so as to reinforce it.
- There is no evidence to suggest that decisions taken on the basis of arbitrary lists lead to more successful long-term relationships.

There is however one crucial difference between the two: in the case of human qualities the judgment, however subjective, is based on current realities, whereas in the Chancellor's case, they are based exclusively on future expectations, some ten, twenty, thirty years down the road. Thus, we are not asked to consider how the City of London is doing outside the Euro - we know she is doing just fine - but what fate holds for her under Frankfurt's financial regime.

We are not asked to compare relative employment prospects within the EU as they are at present, when we know that UK unemployment figures are healthy, well below the EU average and roughly half that of Germany. Instead we are to predict long-term trends once Britain has lost control of the financial instruments designed to influence these very trends.

We are not asked to look at the current state of inward investment, when we know that the UK is by far the leading destination within Europe and that the rate of such investment has grown significantly since the establishment of the Euro. Instead we are to speculate as to where international companies may prefer to locate their subsidiaries in a fast-changing world some decades from now.

We are not asked to examine how convergent the economies of the UK and Europe are at the moment, when we know their cycles are seriously divergent. Instead we must anticipate a date of a likely convergence that can be sustained for all time to come.

We are not asked to measure the degree of flexibility of continental structures, when we know they are far too inflexible to accommodate the traditional British way of doing business. Instead we have to estimate how far any British government would be able to persuade political powers, intent as they are on creating a concentric structure, determined as they are on a process of standardisation and harmonisation, addicted as they are to rules and regulations, to change their basic modus operandi.

We are constantly reminded that economics is not an exact science. This statement is somewhat misleading. Economics, like Psychology, Sociology and History, is no doubt a valuable field of study, but it is neither exact nor inexact science: it is not science at all. As its subject matter concerns the behaviour of human beings, the practical predictive value of the theories it produces is insignificant. If it were able to deliver scientific predictions, investments on the stock exchange would be one-way bets and we could all go home rich and happy. On the first day of January every year, the six or seven leading economic institutions and experts publish a set of precise figures, forecasting key economic indicators over a twelve-month period. They are confined to the UK alone and are to do with relatively straightforward matters such as inflation, interest rates, growth of GDP, exchange rate, etc. Firstly, these forecasts do not agree with each other. Secondly, most of them turn out to be significantly off the mark. Just imagine what the chances are of the Treasury gnomes getting it right, having to deal with at least 15 economies, in the context of much more complex, less well defined criteria, over a period of decades? To base the decision on Euro entry on five such economic "tests", whatever the theory, must surely represent the most gigantic gamble any government has ever proposed in British history.

If, however, we take a more realistic view of the Chancellor's five criteria, demoting their status from that of hard "tests" to "educated guesses", there are some modest conclusions to be derived from considering each one on its merit:

1. There are two kinds of convergence in question, that of business cycles and that of economic structures. Although lumped together, they have nothing to do with each other. Business cycles usually refer to relatively short term phases of fluctuating economies whilst economic structures are about inherent characteristics, slow and difficult to alter. To identify business cycles in retrospect is easy but not when in the midst of one since it requires an accurate prediction of the future. Who could have foreseen a 15-year recession in Japan or an ailing German economy, 5 years after the adoption of the Euro. The relative strengths of independent economies converge and diverge all the time whether they do or do not operate the same currency. In any case, these short-term fluctuations have

no bearing on the fundamental issue. Adopting the Euro is meant to be for good.

Structural convergence, on the other hand, does matter. Here, fortunately, we are on firmer ground. We know that the greater proportion of Britain's international trade, unlike that of other EU countries, is outside the Euro zone and likely to remain so in the foreseeable future. It is also a fact that British firms and families are more vulnerable to interest rate changes than their continental counterparts because of higher levels of home ownership and a preference for variable-rate mortgages. Also, Britain is the only net exporter of oil in the EU; oil price variations, therefore, have a different effect here than on the continent. Even more significantly, Britain does not have a massive un-funded mountain of pension debt casting a menacing shadow over her economy for the next 50 years. Most EU members, and four of the largest, have such levels of debt to current and future state pensioners that they cannot be met without serious inflation or unacceptable hikes in Euro interest rates or, probably, both. There is no prospect of any of these structural factors changing either in Britain or on the continent for the foreseeable future. So the chances of any meaningful long-term economic convergence are slim.

2. To expect a move towards greater flexibility within the EU implies a degree of optimism that surpasses that of those still waiting for Godot. Authorities producing regulations that define the exact parameters of a leek are not exactly in the business of flexibility.

There are two very obvious reasons why structures within the EU will inevitably tend to be less, rather than more, flexible. The first is to do with historic process, the second with national characteristics. An integration-oriented EU is in the process of coming into being, with a growing centre of power. To be successful such a centre must focus on moulding disparate elements into some sort of unity. This means promulgation of new laws, rules and regulations and an emphasis on strict conformity and adherence to them. Only a mature, long-established, secure centre of power can permit itself the luxury of relaxing rules, softening regulations, making exceptions, to become more flexible. The unifying process is inimical, in its very nature, to flexibility. Secondly, neither the German nor the French national character is noted for its flexibility. The history, language, law, values and political culture of these two peoples, at the very heart of an integrationist Europe, lean the other way: towards authority, supremacy of rules, conformity.

The two key areas crucial to flexibility are the labour market and the tax system. Virtually all European legislation affecting the workplace has made the labour market less fluid, less competitive, less able to adapt to ever faster changing economic realities. As for taxation, the integrationist objective is to "harmonise" fiscal policy across the EU, not to cater for the inevitable long-term divergences within it.

3. Long-term investment in a foreign country is governed by a number of obvious considerations: political stability, taxation, cost and quality of labour, communication, ease of doing business, size of the market and the projected future value of the currency. Some of these considerations do not affect the debate. Whether Britain adopts the Euro or not, the labour force and the European market size remain the same. The ease of international communications through the English

language will continue to be hugely attractive. The other factors all matter a great deal. There is no secret as to why foreign firms prefer to put their money here rather than elsewhere in Europe. The Euro zone is in a constant state of political transformation – Britain, so far, is less so. The taxation climate is more benign here than on the continent. Most significant of all, it is simply easier to do business in this country, for any number of reasons, than anywhere else in Europe. Losing Sterling, moving into an integrationist European system, eliminates these crucial advantages in one fell swoop. Foreign capital would find Britain not half as desirable a habitat.

4. The City is now the world's leading financial centre. Interestingly, her pre-eminence is of relatively recent origin, long past the heyday of the British empire, and at a time when the all-powerful Dollar totally eclipsed the Pound. The City's rise had a lot to do with the removal of government restrictions and the gradual elimination of red tape by the Bank of England. What any financial centre needs above all else are a free flow of money and the ease of all transactions encouraging this flow. It is no historical accident that London's precursors, the great banking cities of Genoa, Florence, Venice, Augsburg and Antwerp, flourished when outside the stifling control of the Great Powers of their age. For most of the 16th-century, for example, the highly regimented treasury of mighty Spain was totally in the hands of Genoese bankers and the wars that bankrupted her in 1557 were chiefly financed by the Fuggers' Augsburg bank. This, by the way, was at a time when Spain owned and controlled the lion's share of the world's gold and silver supply! Meanwhile, both Zurich and Geneva continue to flourish, under a tax-benevolent,

confidential and relaxed financial regime, despite the relative unimportance of the Swiss Franc. It is hardly surprising that the Swiss reject not just the Euro but also the EU itself.

Although the European Bank sitting in Frankfurt is supposed to be independent, no one can be under any misapprehension as to the political influence Germany and France will continue to exercise over her style, policies and operations. Neither of these influential powers has a relaxed banking tradition, akin to those of Switzerland, Holland or Britain. Therefore, the Euro-zone is unlikely to offer a viable home for any internationally significant financial centre in the foreseeable future. This is why even the bulk of the new Euro-denominated business is transacted through London, not Frankfurt, or Paris. It requires no great powers of deduction to conclude that it is vital for the future of the City that she retains her freedom and independence, that she remains outside a more tightly regulated Euro-zone, unencumbered by an unstable, unproven currency. More than that, it is actually in the interest of the EU and the Euro, that the strength of Europe's prime financial centre remains unimpaired.

5. The fifth criterion of "higher growth, stability and lasting increase in jobs" is such a hotchpotch that is difficult to take it seriously. Higher growth may run counter to stability and stability sometimes results in loss of jobs. A successful economy, by definition, tends to have good growth, stability and permanence of jobs. So the fifth criterion should read: "Is the economy likely to fare better within a tightly regulated, state inspired, continental political framework or within an enterprise-oriented, less controlled, relatively easy-going, traditional British

model?" The key to this question lies in the character and habits of the British worker, British manager and British businessman. The earlier discussion of national traits, history and culture demonstrates quite clearly why what may function well in concentric Germany and France does not work in eccentric Britain.

Whilst the future well-being of a single European currency is largely a matter of speculation, there are a few certainties to hand to help British deliberations for or against abandoning the Pound. As a member of the Euro zone British input and influence in the conduct of affairs at the Central European Bank would amount to a twelfth or fifteenth or 25th fraction of any decision-making process. It certainly would not be sufficient to materially affect its presidency and style of management that will be firmly under French control for a decade or so. No one seriously claims that interest rates will be set by the ECB to accommodate British needs if they run counter to the needs of Germany or France. In fact, whether Britain joins now or in ten years time, her participation would make precious little difference to the way the Euro is run. On the other hand, the surrender of the Pound would definitely ensure the decline of the Bank of England as an effective force in protecting the specific needs of the British economy and the value of the country's assets. In terms of currency considerations alone, it would be a colossal, indeed a reckless, gamble for Britain to surrender its integral financial instruments in favour of an infant political currency with questionable future prospects.

15

Eastern Promise

When the wind is in the east,
'tis neither good for man nor beast
Seventeenth century proverb

The visionaries of a Greater Europe are not lacking in ambition. With the single currency in place and a federal constitution in the making, enlargement is next on the agenda. For the builders of empires, territorial expansion has always proved irresistible. The geographic limits of the EU in the North, West and South are cogent and well defined. The Arctic, the Atlantic and the Mediterranean seas provide fine natural boundaries. The eastern reaches are something else again. The geography of the continent extends to the Ural mountains and the Caspian sea. The enlargement of the EU is gathering pace, just how far will it stretch? Poland, Slovakia, Hungary, Slovenia, the Czech Republic, the three Baltic states, Cyprus and Malta are now in; various Balkan countries, Bulgaria and Romania are accepted candidates. Turkey, with a projected 100 million Muslim population by 2050, poses a great question mark. How about Moldavia, the Ukraine, Bielorussia, Armenia,

Georgia, Azerbaijan? Will Syria and Iraq be the Union's next-door neighbours? How about Russia herself? Isn't she at least as significant a part of European culture, history and heritage as Montenegro? Have the architects of Greater Europe decided where to draw a rational future border that makes any sense?

The enlargement project may have more immediate ramifications than the Constitution. To the supporters of a Greater Europe it makes no difference. They are rushing simultaneously into both projects with gay abandon. The old ideas of imperialist expansion have taken on a new, politically correct, guise. The drive to add territory, people, markets, resources, to create an instant world power, seems to have blinded politicians as to what is actually being acquired. This impairment is particularly lamentable since awareness of Eastern Europe fundamentals in the West is somewhat sketchy anyway. In conversation, the mention of Transylvania as the country of my origin is invariably followed by a moment or two of uneasy silence whilst people are desperately trying to place it on a hazy, ill-defined mental map of school day memories. "Isn't it where Dracula comes from?" is a favourite cop out. Recently, thousands of British skiers have glided down the slopes of the Carpathians, ten times more have taken advantage of cheap holidays on the shores of the Black Sea, scores of soldiers have patrolled the cities of Bosnia and some intrepid English football fans have had a night out in cities like Katowitze and Kishinev. These brief encounters may have left favourable or unfavourable impressions, but they certainly have not contributed much to any real understanding of the people, their culture, politics and economic circumstance. In the minds of most Britons, all the nations of these diverse regions are lumped together and considered simply as East Europeans.

One would like to believe that in the Foreign Office, in the Quai d'Orsay, in some foreign ministries of other capitals, teams of experts in the ethnography and political history of the continent's eastern reaches, fluent in their languages, having actually lived there for a few years, are at this very moment guiding the enlargement project. Alas, judging by current proceedings, this cannot be so. In true concentric tradition, a rigid, hierarchical set of criteria has been laid down for admission into the EU. Most of the conditions are to do with economic performance and financial status, some with democratic government, some with freedom of speech and basic human rights. The candidate countries have then been classified into *waves*. Those nearest to conforming to the criteria form wave one, those somewhat further behind are part of wave two, and so on. On paper, on an administrative map, this may look meaningful. On the ground, life is nowhere near as neat as that.

We are talking about a population greater than that of France and Britain combined, divided by language, culture, religion, race, geography, national history, political tradition and a complex of other intersecting lines. They have not a great deal in common and often what they share is a legacy of violent conflict, mutual suspicion, a desire to settle old scores and exert national supremacy. The state of affairs in Romania and Hungary, the great divide between them, the political and economic implications of the divide, can serve as an example of the kind of complexities and difficulties the EU is facing in its ambitious embrace of Eastern Europe. I cite it because I have some personal experience of the region. My father served as an officer both in the Hungarian army and the Romanian one. He sat on a city chamber of commerce both under Hungarian and Romanian rule. I learnt the history of my place of birth both in a Romanian and a Hungarian version. I have friends and relations in both countries. I have been back in the region frequently over the last twenty years, both privately and on business, during the communist era and thereafter. I am reasonably well informed.

The Hungarians have more to do with the Japanese than with their Romanian neighbours. Descended from a warrior race, the people are proud, combative, touchy, economical with words, insular, confrontational, rash, short; they typically have a low centre of gravity and high cheek bones to remind them of their Asiatic ancestry. Unlike the Japanese, they are inventive, individualistic, eccentric and difficult to control. They also have a thousand years of well-documented history as well as a rich and distinctive literary culture. Their contribution in the fields of music, science and entertainment is well known in the West. The country is evenly divided between Catholics and Protestants. At the time of the Reformation, the Hungarians produced a variant of their own in the Unitarian church whose teachings have spread well beyond its birthplace. More to the point, centuries of self government and active participation in the management of the Austro-Hungarian empire have prepared the ground for a relatively smooth transition to a democracy on a par with those of many current members of the EU.

Romanian origins are shrouded in mystery. Although the official government line has always claimed a pre-Roman, Dacian ancestry, there is no historical or scientific evidence to justify such a claim. Nor is there, despite a Latin-derived language, any racial link between the Romans and the present inhabitants of the country. A distinct Vlach people certainly lived on the Northern edge of the Ottoman empire in the 17th-century but Romania as a country came into being less than 150 years ago. It had a homogenous peasant population within boundaries roughly half the size of what they are today. In the lottery of Versailles, due to circumstances both tragic and comic, Romania doubled its territory and was handed some 5 million non-Romanians. Ethnic minorities thus constituted one third of the entire population.

In typical Balkan style, the country was initially ruled by an imported German dynasty. Below that a ruling class, wafer-thin, perpetuated an Ottoman tradition of government. Many people consider that tradition to be the epitome of corruption. This is a mistaken view. Corruption implies an honest, healthy system being abused by a number of greedy, cheating officials. The Ottoman method of government, at least from the 18th-century onwards, was wedded to the sale and purchase of administrative offices from the highest to the most humble right across the board. Almost every transaction to do with property, commerce, the law, professional practice, travel, and so on, required official sanction. Every sanction cost money that was pocketed by the officials who passed a portion of it up the line, all the way to the Grand Vizier. The sanction was usually embodied in a document covered in stamps, imprinted from an impressive height by a prized stamper held in the clenched fist of a condescending official. Travelling the continent from west to east one could estimate the distance to Istanbul by the number of stamps required on a permit to proceed. In Romania, to this day, you need multi-stamped permits for most activities. Everything has always been for sale, everybody has always had their price.

The Romanian people are generally friendly, humane, accommodating, helpful, long-suffering and much put upon. They have been miserably exploited all their lives both under home-grown and foreign rule. The omnipresent Orthodox Church has always been an enthusiastic ally of any and every government in power. The richest country in Eastern Europe, with great mineral resources from marble to oil, ample water supply, wonderfully productive soil, a dry Mediterranean climate, mountains covered by primordial forest, almost untouched marshlands, fine sea shores, has been struggling for the last half century to feed her people!

The Communist regime merely aggravated what has always been government by an unrepresentative, autocratic central authority showing sublime disregard for the well being of the country and her people. Under Ceausescu the gap between the fantasy world of officialdom and reality reached gigantic proportions. Whilst the Leader made his daily TV appearance in front of masses of hyperactive workers in mills disgorging endless quantities of steel, and government statistics displayed ever-rising GDP figures, manufacturing plants were rusting away, the infrastructure collapsed, agriculture withered, people starved and the country lay in ruins. The only vibrant sector of the economy was the export of people. Significant quantities of Germans were sold to Germany, Jews to Israel and Hungarians to Hungary. Germans cost a lot, Jews somewhat less, while Hungarians were relatively cheap.

Ceausescu was not brought down by a spontaneous uprising of democratic forces gathering strength underground. The decisive movement that led to his fall originated with the courageous defiance of a single Hungarian pastor in Transylvania and a devoted congregation that threw a protective ring around him. Unfortunately, not a great deal has changed since 1989. The same governing establishment, the same judiciary, chiefs of police, hierarchy of functionaries, are in office today and continue to exercise their power in much the same way as before. Any enduring democracy must be rooted in a benign, sophisticated political culture. In Romania the prospect of such a culture is light years away.

There is now more food available, the media is less censored and minorities have some nominal rights to representation and, within limits, the use of their mother tongue. But ever since 1919, the total assimilation of the five million ethnic foreigners bequeathed by the Versailles Treaty, has been the main preoccupation of Romanian politics. This is most evident in Transylvania with her two million Hungarians still unassimilated, still living there. The dominant parties, the loudest voices in the course of the last three elections, have been those of the ex-communists and the ultra nationalists. Statues of Antonescu, the fascist wartime leader who aided and abetted the extermination of some 300,000 Jews, erected in the last decade, still stubbornly defy a parliamentary act decreeing their removal.

There is, however, another ethnic problem, more intractable, more submerged that affects not only Romania but most of her neighbours too. To talk plainly of gypsies in today's political parlance is well nigh impossible. People in this country have a rather romantic idea of a Romany race whose sons and daughters wander freely about the countryside in pleasantly painted, horse-drawn caravans, dancing the flamenco and playing sentimental tunes on ancient violins. Nobody can say with any accuracy just how many gypsies inhabit Eastern Europe. They live outside the parameters of the settled population and form an invisible economy within the black economy that cannot be measured. They shun authority and easily outwit any census. According to the World Bank they are Europe's fastest growing ethnic minority. Low estimates put the figure around six million, with perhaps one half living in Romania, the rest dispersed in Hungary, Slovakia, Moldavia, Bulgaria and ex-Yugoslav countries. They do not consider themselves bound by state laws. Their children are brought up in sporadic contact with state educational systems. Births, marriages and deaths are unregistered. Hygiene is poor, living conditions dismal, petty crime endemic. If they are employed, it is as temporary casual labour. In urban areas, you may see them move in largish bands engaged in activities that range from aggressive begging to stealing and mugging. They are despised, hated, feared and hostile. The Social Affairs Commissioner of the EU has admitted that the resources of the EU states are insufficient to tackle the Roma problem. As an ethnic minority permanently on the fringes of society, they constitute a massive headache to the governments of all countries affected. In Romania, because of the numbers involved and the nature of the country, gypsies are a permanent, irreducible reality.

Livia Jaroka, elected in May 2004 in Hungary, is the first Gypsy member of the European Parliament. In her own words: "In Eastern Europe many Roma live in squalid ghettos with no running water, suffering partial starvation and a short life expectancy...Brussels had been very good at pressuring new EU members to address the Roma issue but failed to take concrete action itself....the new EU countries have been very good at satisfying the wishes of Brussels, adopting formal anti-discrimination legislation, but Roma people do not actually feel the effect of it..." She should know what she is taking about. If the Union was serious about the treatment of ethnic minorities, those countries concerned should not have been allowed to join before the problem was sorted. Legislation itself is not very meaningful if not strictly enforced. Now the misery of these millions falls within the province of the Union where Ms Jaroka is working to set up a special department of Roma affairs. With Romania and Bulgaria set to join in 2007 the prospects of this department could not be any rosier. The same cannot be said of the Roma themselves whose living standards will only improve with migration west.

Erstwhile Yugoslavia's bloody dissolution should have demonstrated once more both the futility and danger of creating artificial political constructs out of complex ingredients by remote international bodies. Why should the incorporating of Bosnia, Serbia, Croatia, Macedonia, Montenegro, Albania and Kosovo into a vastly enlarged EU solve their little local difficulties? How exactly can Brussels so instantly succeed where Versailles so spectacularly failed? Other than vague, benign generalities none of the architects of a Greater Europe has attempted to provide an intelligible answer.

Czechoslovakia, another unfortunate progeny of Versailles, fell apart because the Czech inhabitants of

Bohemia and Moravia have a history, culture and religion that bears little relation to those of the people inhabiting the northern Carpathian mountains. For centuries Prague has been a magnificent seat of European civilisation. The Czechs are, for some reason, the only people with a genuine democratic instinct in the whole of central Europe. Typically, in attempting to defend their religious liberties and autonomous rights in face of Hapsburg demands in 1618, they did not kill the Emperor's envoys, merely defenestrated them. Responsibility for the ensuing Thirty Years War can hardly be laid at their door (or window). The Slovaks, in comparison, after many centuries of Hungarian domination, have no history of self-government and their political culture is rudimentary.

Democratic credentials and living standards hardly improve going further north and east. Conformity to minimum EU requirements becomes increasingly questionable, meaningful convergence is by no means assured. Any statistics emerging in these areas cannot be taken at face value. If there is one thing all these nations learned during the communist era, it was the art of window dressing. Merely to survive, everyone, from the humblest manufacturing unit to the largest ministry, had to churn out a stream of records, reports and statistics to match or exceed government prescriptions. If the monthly rate of chair production was set at 700 pieces, come what may, 700 chairs appeared on paper. Whether 700 people had something to sit on, and for how long, and in what comfort, was a secondary consideration.

The fine print in the European's Commission's own 2003 report states that Poland, for example, was in violation of EU rules on pollution, water control, food safety, fisheries and farming. She lacked the means to deliver EU subsidies and, even more fatally, the country did not have a political, administrative and business culture to resist corruption. Very few of the ten new member states have in fact met the entry criterion of having a functioning market economy that could withstand the competitive pressures of a common market. No doubt, all this will be put right miraculously in a few short years. No doubt Polish pigs can fly. All candidate countries will always supply the EU on time with the right statistics to meet targets set. No doubt the commission will be presented with just the right evidence to demonstrate flourishing human rights and the wonderful state of ethnic minorities, whose allegiance has been miraculously transferred to their adopted nation. The relentless expansion eastwards is set to continue with the underlying realities being suppressed long enough to sanction entry.

After thirteen years of unification, East Germany is still a world away from her Western counterpart. Its costs are bringing Germany to her knees. The expense of bringing the eastern states into line with current EU members will be incalculably greater and the time scale is of a different magnitude. Why not enlarge the Union by easy stages, more gradually, with individual countries admitted on merit, not as part of a typical European grandiose gesture. In an ideal world, one would naturally wish to extend the benefits of an unprecedented prosperity, freedom and justice we enjoy in the West across the entire continent. In the long-term it is highly desirable that this should come to pass. The prospect of joining the larger community may have an immediately beneficial effect, tending to accelerate the improvements that are needed to make such a move a success. But enlargement should be a natural, organic process, allowed to take time, so that any given country admitted to the EU will have already conformed to its norm. The Czech Republic, Hungary and Slovenia seem a reasonable bet, some other recent entrants far from that. The ten countries have a GDP less than half of the EU average and the attractive subsidies they are all expecting are unaffordable. Unaffordable, that is, unless the French are prepared to give up some of theirs, which is highly unlikely. The theory of waves may work well in theoretical physics. As a system of European growth, it may turn out to be a disaster.

The issue of the Union's eastern border will not just go away. Unresolved, it will come back to haunt us from the moment the process of enlargement becomes a fact. The threat to European civilisation, from the Visigoths to the Soviets, has always come from the East. The danger is still from the same quarter and is as real as it ever was. Hundreds of millions of people work hard to eke out a modest living, endure arbitrary, unstable, irrational government, are deprived of the means to improve their lot and eye with longing and envy the freedoms, comforts and sheltered lives enjoyed by fellow human beings right across their border. In the past 20 years, migration from Eastern to Western Europe has taken the form of not just Poles, Hungarians and others moving into EU countries but Ukrainians and Romanians flocking on to Hungarian building sites and Polish farms. This population movement from the East will be a permanent feature of this century since the huge differentials in living standards are unlikely to even out in the foreseeable future.

Britain, more than any country within the EU, is the

favoured final destination of the eastern migrant. She has the most indulgent asylum and immigration policies, the most accessible welfare services, the fairest legal system, the greatest degree of tolerance, full employment and, above all else, a language that is fast becoming universal property. This migration, as some others in the past, is bound to bring great benefits to the country. Many of the entrants are talented, industrious, ambitious and enterprising. They will make a telling contribution to the academic, economic and social life of Britain. At the same time, at least in the short term, they will make additional demands on the country's limited resources. Applications to British universities from students in the new member states more than doubled the year of the enlargement, bringing the EU total to over 20,000. These students have to be treated on a par with home undergraduates, reducing the tuition fees from up to £16,000 to a maximum of £1,125. A great portion of these fees will be paid by the state, in any case, since parental income in the new member countries will often be less than £21,475. The same sort of equation applies, of course, to the NHS and social services.

As long as the massive economic disparities within Europe persist, the issue of temporary barriers between states is unavoidable. In the absence of easily controlled natural boundaries in the East, the states that form the effective border should be homogeneous, strong, dependable, with a settled form of government and relatively free of corruption. They must have the will and the means to police a fragile border both in terms of human and commercial traffic. Porous boundaries will place a burden on the EU that it simply cannot survive. "Almost every one of the new member states in Central and Eastern

Europe will become source, transit and destination countries for criminal goods and services" warns a stark 27-page Europol report. This should sound alarm bells for the few European leaders still keeping an open mind.

There is, however, one other serious complication inherent in any enlargement. It may be possible to enlarge the EU, it may be possible to move towards political integration, it may even be possible for the nations of the continent to retain a significant portion of their independence. What is palpably impossible is to do all three at the same time. They are incompatible. With 25 constituent member states integration becomes harder. With integration moving apace, national rights disappear. If national decision-making is to be protected, integration must fall by the wayside. It is useful to bear in mind that the political establishments within the EU are collectively attempting just precisely this: to enlarge, integrate and preserve the nation states concurrently. They are trying to accomplish the impossible.

16

Superpower versus Sovereignty

Yes, it is Europe, from the Atlantic to the Urals,
it is the whole of Europe, that will decide
the fate of the world
Charles De Gaulle

The Greater Europe dream is one of a state with a population of some 450 million, a gross domestic product approaching that of the States, a currency rivalling the Dollar and a dominant player in the international arena. The attraction lies in the sheer size of such an enterprise. On the face of it, size does matter. Smaller nations living under the shadow of sizeable neighbours have never had an easy time of it, as the histories of Poland, Portugal, Ireland and Finland exemplify. In fact, we are constantly threatened by just such a scenario: Britain, on its own, dwarfed by a continental colossus. But for size to count, to punch its weight, it must be linked to other, qualitative attributes. All Great Powers in history, from the Roman Empire to the Soviet Union, have exhibited some basic common characteristics. A comparison with the European Union is instructive:

- A single geographic centre, where all power is concentrated, and from where all power flows. *Far from having one geographic centre, the European Union already has three official ones: the administration in Brussels, the parliament in Strasbourg, the bank in Frankfurt, in addition to Paris and Berlin, where many key decisions are customarily taken.*
- A single principal language, serving both as an official and a practical channel of communication. *Although English is fast becoming the lingua franca of the world, all official documents within the EU come in at least seventeen languages.*
- A set of political institutions, related to each other in terms of a clearly defined, single hierarchy. *The relationships between Brussels, Strasbourg, national governments and parliaments are less, rather than more, clearly defined with the passing of every new European directive. The proposed constitution enshrines multiple political institutions, competing for decision-making powers.*
- A single set of laws observed uniformly throughout the entire territory. *Laws and modes of legislation are deeply embedded in national cultures; it is difficult to see how they can be standardised without destroying the cultures themselves.*
- A single legislative body to enact and modify this set of laws. *In addition to the Brussels Commission and the European Parliament, each national parliament generates, and will continue to generate, its own legislation.*

- Armed forces, under unified command and with a common code of conduct, for external protection. *Allied armies have quite often fought battles under unified command but an EU integrated army would amount to something akin to the French Foreign Legion, with national allegiances totally submerged. Is this a practical option?*
- A common ideology, embraced democratically or imposed undemocratically. *There is no discernible common European ideology, comparable, for example, to the Pax Romana or to Marxism. There are just vague, abstract ideals, lofty affirmations of democratic principles and human rights. The reality is endless bickering inspired by narrow national self-interest.*
- A willingness by the people at the grass roots to tolerate the dominion of the centre. *In Mediterranean countries the compliance of people with the directives of their own governments is fitful enough. How much more tenuous will it be when central power is in the hands of strangers in a foreign land, hundreds of kilometres away.*
- Growth from a small central core, by conquest, marriage or economic expansion, into a greater geopolitical entity. *No Great Power so far in history has come into being by a voluntary, planned amalgamation of a number of medium-sized states. The Roman Empire grew out of a tiny state around Rome. The British Empire evolved from "Little England". Japan was unified in wars of conquest by dominant tribes centred on Kyoto. Modern Germany owes her existence to Otto von Bismarck*

riding the success of Prussian arms to create a Greater Prussia. The United States of America, stemming from the emancipation of 13 British Colonies, occupying a narrow strip of land on her Atlantic seaboard, perhaps comes closest, but still light years away from the emerging pattern of the EU.

It is fairly obvious that Europe is not likely to become a Great Power within anybody's lifetime. Of all the prerequisites, homogeneity of culture, fostered by a unified code of legal, social and economic practice, a single centre of power, are the most essential. The centre of power must speak with all the authority of a single voice, whether the authority is democratically derived, as in the case of Roosevelt and Churchill or self acquired, as in the case of Napoleon, Hitler and Stalin.

The fact that a European Superpower is a distant dream will not deter political establishments from having a go at it. At least on the continent it is recognised that the Greater Europe project requires the establishment of a European code of practice in all spheres that matter and the homogenising of political structures throughout the continent. It is openly admitted that nation states have to give up a significant portion of their decision-making powers and radically alter current practices. What is on offer is, at the very least, a power-sharing deal. Let there be no mistake about that.

It is plainly dishonest to pretend that you can have the one without the other: to have the benefits of being part of a Great Power and retain your national integrity. Only too often, European enthusiasts here, Kenneth Clarke, Chris

Patten, Robin Cook, Leon Brittan, Charles Kennedy, Michael Heseltine, Tony Blair, Peter Mandelson and others right across party divides, talk about *strengthening, broadening, building up* the EU into a greater and greater powerhouse, as simply a beneficial *addition* to Britain's existing state. Their language reminds one of a sales pitch promoting a deal that is supposed to result in *incremental income:* no additional work, no outlay, no further risks, no increase in overheads, just some extra profit. In the real world, as we well know, there are very few pure gains. The power to decide is finite. It does not grow or multiply. If you divide it, delegate it, or pool it, this power is diluted. A decision taken by Devon County Council, or by the Edinburgh Assembly or at a EU summit, or in Brussels, is a decision *not* taken at Westminster. There is simply no escaping the fact that Britain's sovereignty is at stake.

But what does sovereignty really mean? In one sense, it is simply having a flag, an anthem, a more or less well defined territory, a head of state, an army, a police force, a national bank, usually with its own currency and, as importantly, international recognition. In this sense, Poland, Hungary, East Germany, were all sovereign states before the collapse of the Soviet Union. In another sense, a more meaningful one, they were not sovereign states. Despite having all the *formal* attributes of independence, they lacked its very essence. Their armies obeyed the commands of the Warsaw Pact; their ideologies and laws were formulated in Moscow; their codes of practice and economic structures were integrated into that of the Soviet bloc. Critically, they lost the power to make their own decisions in almost every sphere of national life.

Admittedly, this was the result of a foreign invasion and

Britain is not on the verge of being physically occupied. But the peril is all the greater for that. For instead of a hostile military force, the threat is a subtle, insidious erosion of Britain's independent decision-making powers. And as long as the EU keeps growing in size, integration and centralisation, this process is both inevitable and irreversible. A Greater Europe *means* harmonisation, standardisation, homogenisation of commerce, finance, industry, codes of practice, laws, administration, institutions and finally of the relationship between the individual and the state. It is simply not manageable otherwise. We have witnessed every ministerial summit bring in its wake some transfer of decision-making authority from individual states to a European administrative body. A veto or two surrendered here, a few extensions of Brussels' domain there, all add up over the years to a steady erosion of the country's independence.

This process of erosion has a number of clearly identifiable sources:

- A conscious drive by political elites towards integration.
- The natural momentum of the centralising trend.
- The tendency of Brussels, as any administrative centre, to grow in strength and enlarge its decision-making domain.
- The need to compromise underlying principles in the interest of short-term solutions.
- The unintended consequences of any legislation that go beyond its original purpose. Thus, for example, European law puts the onus on the employer to prove non-discrimination in the

workplace, undercutting one of the fundamentals of British justice: the presumption of innocence.

The way this power transfer works is historically unique and has most peculiar consequences. At the base of the project there is a general consensus among continental political elites that integration requires ever greater standardisation and centralisation of authority. The operational arm of the EU in Brussels, on its own initiative, produces outline proposals in all areas of economic, social, legal, financial and political activity still, up to this point, within the province of national parliaments. These proposals are generally agreed at summits or other high level ministerial meetings by the national governments. Those with reservations or opposed are being assuaged by the thought that these outline proposals would be radically modified before final approval. Now Brussels comes really into its own, drafting detailed directives as only a bureaucracy well schooled in the Napoleonic traditions can. Each and every one of them is formulated to extend as far as possible the scope of the Union, to accentuate its control, to transfer powers from the individual nations to a European central authority. For this is the essence of the whole exercise. These directives, now virtually in their final form, are submitted once again to national governments in a manner to ensure that meaningful modifications are minimised. The detailed directives are then formally approved on the nod at the next pressurised meeting of Heads of Government where headline topics of immediate political moment take always natural precedence.

Up to this stage in the process the national parliaments have been kept on the margins if not totally ignored. Now that the European directives are set in stone, it is the duty of national parliaments to enact laws such that give these directives legal status within each country's own legislature. Thus parliaments, considered sovereign hitherto, have become, at least in part, the subservient organs of an un-elected central authority. And as the greater portion of laws passed by national parliaments over the last decade simply enshrine EU directives, the loss of sovereignty is simply a fact.

When it comes to giving effect to these laws, to reconciling the daily life of people to their intended or unintended ramifications, to meeting the costs they inevitably incur, to policing the manifold rules and regulations they generate, Brussels need not lift a finger: all of it has to be shouldered by the individual nations. This is the beauty of the integrationist enterprise: with an administration smaller than that of an average English county and a budget a mere fraction of that of the member states in their totality, a central authority is insidiously acquiring enough power to aspire to the government of an entire continent.

The EU, as presently constituted, represents something of a halfway house between a Europe of independent nations and a European federal state. The source of the bulk of legislation is central, most of the citizen rights are Union-wide, the European Court of Justice is vying for supremacy with national courts and the European Parliament is flexing its muscles whilst actual compliance with the laws and regulations generated by the centre are administered by the constituent states, each following its own bent, national interest and individual custom. Such a structure is inherently unstable. The Union has to integrate further or retrench its powers. The extension of the Eurozone and the adoption of the draft European Constitution would definitely tilt the balance. Consequently, the Euro has assumed in the public mind a meaning beyond just money. It has come to stand for the independence already lost, the independence at stake now and the independence that will be lost in the future, if the process of integration goes on unhindered. This is why the Danes, despite the combined pressure of all the political parties and the media, voted to retain the Danish Krone. And why the Swedes followed suit.

What makes the European Constitution so dangerous to the survival of the nation state is that it will serve as a vehicle for the integrationist forces to draw a federation of states ever closer. Whatever its final text, aided and abetted by Brussels, there will be a continuous stream of amendments, interpretations, clarifications and extensions to cement central authority. None of these will, in themselves, be remarkable but their cumulative effect may well make the political fabric of later 21st-century Britain unrecognisable to her present inhabitants. The political parties debate as to who lost a greater portion of British sovereignty so far: Labour or Tories. It does not matter a jot whether the chief culprit is Heath, Wilson, Thatcher, Major or Blair. What those people who care about the country's independence must ensure is that this insidious process of erosion is brought to an abrupt halt.

17

A Meaningful Foreign Policy

"What matters it how far we go?" his scaly friend replied.
"There is another shore, you know, upon the other side.
The further off from England the nearer is to France -
Then turn not pale, beloved snail,
but come and join the dance"
Lewis Carroll
Alice's Adventure in the Wonderland

Britain has not had a foreign policy for the best part of a century. With the loss of her imperial vision, reactions replaced actions and clear strategies withered into disconnected tactical moves. The nation's heroic performance in World War Two and the dismantling of an extensive empire were major historic achievements, but they left Britain's place in a transformed world undefined. The creation of a Commonwealth served merely as a transitional stage and her relations with an emerging political entity in Europe were characterised by a lack of foresight, an absence of clear objectives. This was in stark contrast with the French who, in the space of one generation, turned their defeated and morally devastated country into the dominant political force on the continent.

If the people of the British Isles are to retain their political culture and safeguard their independence within a continent currently led by concentric forces, it is imperative to have a European strategy that delineates Britain's relations with the United States, the Commonwealth and Europe, all in the context of a rapidly changing world. On the face of it, for Britain to develop a meaningful foreign policy is not an easy task. The so-called special relationship with the US is asymmetric and cannot be one of equals. The Commonwealth is weak. As an island on the North Western edge of Europe, representing one eighth of her population, it is hard to envisage Britain assuming the central role within the continent. Some commentators never tire of reiterating that she is in danger of losing out in each of these alliances, falling between three stools and ending up in splendid isolation.

On a closer look, the reality is not quite as unpromising as that. Being the most significant ally of the world's sole superpower, Britain still retains not inconsiderable influence on the global stage. This was ably demonstrated by Maggie Thatcher when Iraq invaded Kuwait, by John Major during the Gulf War and by Tony Blair since 9/11. Militarily and economically supreme, the US faces all the difficulties associated with such dominance. Although unchallenged by any rival power, wide ranging economic and strategic interests render the US vulnerable to relatively minor forces and events outside her boundaries and beyond her direct control. She is dependent on an uninterrupted flow of oil from the Middle East, on key industrial components and manufactured goods from the Far East and a massive supply of foreign money to fund the chronic deficit in her trade with the rest of the world.

The same dominance will inevitably make an already unloved America ever more unpopular. The apparent triumph of an "unfettered" free market system brings in its wake dangerous hostilities. The lifting of the Communist threat, the rescuing of Europe from one dictatorship or another over the last hundred years are long forgotten and do not seem to count for much outside the Anglo-Saxon world. The French cultural establishment, dominated, as always, by the Left, has long despised and resented the much coarser, mass-market American imports. Its political counterpart, vying for power, instinctively protectionist, has been a thorn in the flesh throughout global trade negotiations and obstructive at the Security Council of the UN. At least one German minister has had the nerve to draw a parallel between Bush and Hitler. Joshka Fischer, in control of Foreign Relations, has been an ardent and active anti-capitalist all his life and the current Chancellor used the anti-American card shamelessly to scrape back into power in the course of the last general election. Japanese and American mentalities are fundamentally irreconcilable, so no kinship between the two nations is possible. In her foreign affairs the US has consistently displayed a certain naivety, a lack of local sensitivity, a lack of imagination and subtlety. She has a perilous tendency to oversimplify. For all these reasons, as demonstrated most recently in the shambles of post-war Iraq, the US badly needs a dependable, trustworthy, effective friend. Britain is the only country able to fulfil this role. The two nations have a closely interwoven history, share a language, an eccentric political culture and have been natural allies for over one hundred years.

What Britain brings to the alliance should not be under-estimated. London is likely to remain the pre-eminent international financial centre. In quantitative terms, British arms can contribute little to the mighty US military machine. On the other hand, armed intervention in the world's trouble spots most often requires not so much an overwhelming force as smaller, specialised, highly trained units deployed with great rapidity. Britain is well equipped to do that. She is also indispensable to the NATO alliance, which is still a key element of the US global defensive strategy. Beyond that, British political leadership, at its strongest, provides a unique two-way link between America and Europe in almost every sphere. The two relatively civilised and moderately democratic halves of the West constitute a small minority of the global population. They must, at the end of the day, act as one. The threat posed by the overwhelming majority, those less fortunate, less politically stable, less predictable, is simply just too acute to ignore.

In recent conflicts - the Balkans, the Gulf, Afghanistan, Iraq – Britain acted in a pivotal role bringing together America and some European countries in effective coalitions. It is safe to assume that international crises will occur more often and have greater impact than in the past. But even in areas like free trade or the environment that seldom give rise to crises, British influence tends to inform and moderate entrenched positions on both sides of the Atlantic. This is largely due to Britain being something of a half-way house between Europe and America in matters touching on the economic, political and cultural life of society. Situated somewhere in between a rampant free market and a highly regulated system, between a historically old, conservative world and one thriving on constant movement and accelerating change, Britain has a unique vantage point. Just as the greatest threat to Europe is from the East, so the most powerful forces set to influence life on this continent in the foreseeable future are likely to come from the West. Developments in economic activity and innovation in popular culture tend to be generated in America, with Britain following closely behind. American business methods, Hollywood films, MacDonald hamburgers, non-stop litigation, computer games and the rest of the invasive imports from over there may not be welcome or desirable but they are, for better or worse, a fact of life.

The value to this country derived from a close friendship with the US is fairly obvious. Enhanced international stature, inward investment, opportunities of shared technology, exchange of intelligence, military collaboration, are some of the benefits among a host of others. British political influence in the formation and implementation of US foreign policy is often derided. Yet this input is likely to keep pace with the globalisation of conflict, utilisation of human and natural resources, ideological and religious divides, the collapse of law and order. Fewer and fewer are any of these issues locally confined. There is, as always, a downside. British prime ministers will be regularly caricatured as poodles of American presidents. The German and French political establishments will continue to accuse Britain of betraying European interests at every convenient opportunity, but then they do this anyway. More importantly, alignment with the US will make this country a prime terrorist target, but this is a price that has to be paid. Yet, all in all, a meaningful Anglo-American dimension to any British foreign policy is a given. This alliance, unlike European ones, is not embodied in any formal treaty, joint institutions, higher courts or a supra-national constitution. It is simply an understanding between two peoples with shared history, approach and values. It has stood the test of time and is likely to survive changes in government, presidential elections and political orientation of various parties. It is a natural alliance of nations, not a deal concluded between politicians.

The Commonwealth, although a diminishing asset, is not without some meaning in the greater scheme of things. The now sovereign nations of what was once an empire no longer form a cohesive entity. Australia has little in common with Zambia, or Canada with the Indian sub-continent. Realistically, Britain is just not strong enough to hold together such disparate countries, with divergent interests and political cultures. If the entire Commonwealth cannot bring enough pressure to dislodge a petty despot like Mugabe, it does not amount to much. At the same time, the parts, taken separately, are of greater value than the whole.

Britain has even stronger links to Australia, New Zealand and Canada, than to the US. Kinship, language, history and shared values are a strong foundation of an instinctive alliance. More than that, the geo-political situation of these countries is somewhat analogous to that of Britain. The Far East is essential to the economic development of Australia and New Zealand. It also poses a serious threat to their distinctive identity. Exactly the same applies to Canada in relation to the US. The opportunities and dangers of being located on the edge of a vastly greater continent leads to an ambivalent attitude to it, as exemplified by Britain's natural reserve towards mainland Europe. In a global context, British foreign policy cannot afford to neglect such valuable potential allies merely as a consequence of her membership of the EU.

The remnants of a colonial past in Africa and Asia, varied as they are, have also something in common. It is politically correct to display feelings of guilt in respect of the commercial exploitation of these countries, past treatment of their inhabitants and national divides left behind. A measure of such feeling, looking back from today's society to another historical period, is understandable. It is less fashionable, but more relevant, to look at the other side of the same coin. The administrative machinery, the infrastructure, the legal framework, great chunks of industry and commerce and what democracy still survives, is also British colonial legacy. So is the education system and, in most cases, the country's official language. It is natural therefore, that in matters of higher education, military, economic and technological support most of these Commonwealth countries tend to gravitate to Britain. Maintaining these relationships draws on the country's resources but it also offers substantial opportunities to British industry and commerce. These links also translate into a political influence across the world not shared by any other member of the EU with the exception, and to a much lesser degree, of France.

The time has come to define an active foreign policy for the New Commonwealth. Such a policy will not be based just on responding to hunger, disease, violent local conflict and natural disaster, wherever they occur. It will not lump together millions of people under one undifferentiated humanitarian umbrella. Rather, on the lines of the American "favoured nations" principle, such a policy would promote and encourage relations with each country in the measure that she, in turn, embraced a power-sharing form of government, achieved stability, reciprocated British support and helped further British interests. To those living in an affluent society able to afford liberal principles, such a foreign policy may seem selfish. Experience of the real world, unfortunately, teaches that no other policy works.

But it is in relation to Europe that a lack of clear-sighted foreign policy objectives since World War Two hurt Britain most. In the same period, the French and German leadership, in stark contrast, pursued a single, well-defined strategy. With the rise of de Gaulle and the post-war renaissance of German industry, the agenda was set, its terms followed with single-minded determination. For over a century and a half successive attempts by each one of the two states to establish a political hegemony over the mainland continent failed in wars that resolved nothing whilst draining the continent of its manhood, energy and moral certainties. The lesson learnt by the respective political establishments, significantly, was not to give up their aim but to share it within the framework of a joint domination of the European continent. One has to admit that to a remarkable extent they have realised this objective. In the good old-fashioned concentric tradition, the Presidents of France and the Chancellors of Germany get down to settle the major affairs of the continent in private prior to having their decisions endorsed by the lesser members of the European community. Following de Gaulle and Adenauer, Pompidou and Brandt, Schmidt and Giscard d'Estaing, Mitterrand and Kohl, the duo of Chirac and Schröder continued this excellent tradition in the privacy of a Copenhagen hotel, in the late spring of 2003, to the chagrin of Tony Blair, by making a deal on the CAP and enlargement just prior to the summit convened specifically to discuss these very subjects.

De Gaulle saw clearly the importance of keeping Britain out of the Common Market, deeming, quite rightly, Britain to belong to an Anglo-Saxon world, whose political culture is somewhat removed from that of France or what the French consider as Europe. Whilst the French political establishment constructed a European Union in its own image, its British counterpart was at times asleep and at times engaged elsewhere. When it eventually woke up to what was happening right on its doorstep, a period of disorientation set in. When it comes to European relations, British governments have been pathetically indecisive, politicians ambiguous, leaders ineffective and parties divided both within and against each other. Each unfolding move towards an integrated continent has thrown the political world here into fresh turmoil, with petty domestic infighting and personal vituperation displacing rational thought and peripheral vision.

The Great Deception tells the story of the European Union from its visionary inception to the constitution of a Greater Europe. Written by Christopher Booker and Richard North, the book is a dry, factual account of how Monnet's dream of an integrated Europe came to be translated into a political reality. Treaty by treaty, summit by summit, the tale reveals the same essential elements: the powerful driving force of an ideological and committed political elite; a voracious central administration in Brussels; the sublime diplomatic skills of the French, ever vigilant, proactive and ready to take advantage of every opportunity to strengthen their country's dominant position; the dismal ignorance, unpreparedness and superficiality of the British politicians concerning all matters touching the Union and the pathetic performance of the Foreign Office throughout the entire process. Reading the book one is left with the impression of a European master class conducted by French professors with British pupils arriving always late, ill prepared, their contribution confined to ineffectual protests. *The Great Deception* is a seminal work that ought to be mandatory reading material to all MPs, MEPs, Peers, political commentators and whoever means to participate seriously in the European debate.

One of the sources of the confusion in this country, if indeed not the main one, has been the identification of the Franco-German axis and its offspring, the EU regime, with the European continent. They are not one-and-the-same thing. It is no surprise that many people in this country, fed up with the goings-on in Brussels and disillusioned by manipulative summitries, have become Euro-sceptics. The British political establishment itself, so naïve when it comes to the continent, has largely resigned itself to Franco-German domination and to the existing management style of the EU. Thus, facing the forces of integration, all Britain has had to offer so far, is reluctance, resistance and refusal: on their own, not very promising ingredients for an active foreign policy.

The major European wars over the previous two centuries revolved round a Franco-German axis. Now that this axis is one no longer of conflict but an active alliance, it is suddenly acclaimed as the very foundation of a blissful continent, at peace with itself for all time to come. To see it thus is to take a superficial, misleadingly dangerous point of view. However the responsibility for those major wars is apportioned, and debates on that subject will never cease, they could not have arisen without the impelling drive of concentric societies governed by an authoritarian leadership. The principal danger of armed conflict in Europe lies not in instinctive national antipathies or diverse economic interests, but in the competing ambitions of concentric governments. The good news is that the Franco-German axis is not in conflict just now. The bad news is that such an axis is still there at all. The disconcerting news is that the hopes of a new European dawn are pinned on it. So long as ultimate decision-making powers are held in very few hands and are easily imposed on people with centuries' old habits of compliance, the long-term political stability of the continent must remain in doubt.

Admittedly, the Franco-German alliance has been effective and served the post-war interests of the two nations well. It helped to rehabilitate German industry and eased her people into the European community. It brought France the political leadership of the EU. But are the factors that brought the alliance into being still in place today? Is the determination to sustain the deal between them as strong as at the outset? The German vision of a truly federal political structure for the continent entails national sacrifices that the French, when it comes down to it, find hard to swallow. Thus far, France has had to give up remarkably little. With her political establishment in effective control of the EU, transfer of powers from Paris to Brussels has been relatively easy. Not many mourned the loss of a perennially weak Franc. In financial terms France has always been a net beneficiary and her agricultural base has continued to enjoy unparalleled protection. The enlargement of the EU and a politically less submissive Germany inevitably weakens the French hold on Brussels. At the same time the momentum of further integration tends to open up protected French markets and loosen government control over subsidised industry.

In Germany's case, the change is more dramatic. To all intents and purposes Germany is now rehabilitated. Germans are still not universally liked but they are no longer considered enemies in the eyes of their neighbours. The war ghosts have been, more or less, exorcised. The political establishment feels under no further obligation to shore up French agriculture. The general public is beginning to resent openly the one-way flow of their money into the ever expanding but porous coffers of Brussels. The surrender of the treasured Mark for the unpopular Euro has raised additional doubts in the public mind about the value of the French alliance. Of greater moment still, the German industrial giant of the last five decades has entered the 21st century suddenly all wobbly. The engine that was supposed to drive the economy of the entire continent is proving so weak that it can barely drag along its own ailing self. This weakness, moreover, does not appear to be a mere hiccup in an otherwise streamlined operation. Large swathes of endemic unemployment, stagnation, lack of competitiveness, sharply declining business confidence, shrinking investment, consumer resistance are all ominous signs. The burden of East Germany, of the EU and the Euro currency, a rigid and overprotected labour force, a generous welfare state and stifling regulations are the ingredients of a potent cocktail to debilitate Germany for at least a decade to come.

To see obvious signs, to analyse causes does not necessarily mean that the country is ready to accept profound changes, that a make over is in the offing. Beyond what is visible and easily understood, there are factors at play that make the prospect of a German renaissance not very promising. We are now at least two generations away from those men and women who by grim determination and self-sacrifice revived the fortunes of a defeated, destroyed, occupied country. The terrible twins of success and affluence have made the present generation complacent, self-centred, defensive. The famed German work ethic ain't what it used to be. At the same time, global patterns of economic activity have radically changed too. The role of heavy industry, like ship building, car production, machine tools and so on, has declined. The emphasis has shifted to a new world of information technology, fashion, marketing, entertainment, a world less dependent on the German virtues of long-term planning, systematic approach and discipline. It now relies more on initiative, spontaneity, flexibility and flair, qualities the Germans famously lack. Germany is in danger of being out of tune with world economic trends. This is not to say that Germany is doomed. Although recent statistical analysis of comparative birth rates and therefore available work forces predicts that Britain's GDP will overtake that of Germany by 2040 she is still an economic powerhouse and the essential base of the Euro currency. But she is not a colossus, not even the determining factor for the future economic shape of Europe.

For all these reasons, the Franco-German axis is not a source of strength but the continent's greatest weakness.

On many specific issues, the CAP, liberalisation of markets, free trade, Brussels administration, some key aspects of the Constitution, the two allies appear to be at odds. What holds the axis together is the desperation of the political establishment of both countries to hang on jointly to the levers of EU power. They are still at one in their compulsive imposition of home grown concentric habits of government on the entire European continent.

If this analysis is only half correct, British foreign policy in relation to Europe defines itself. Its primary objective, its long-term strategy has to be the harnessing of all the eccentric forces within the continent in a voluntary move towards a genuine European Democracy. The need is for people to have the same sense of belonging, of participating in decision making, of being individually valued, as they have in this country. Such an agenda, of course, is the opposite of what is being tabled now. It is not about Britain joining a Greater Europe, it is about a more modest Europe joining, in profound political terms, Britain. The struggle between the concentric and eccentric forces for the soul of Europe is taking place right now and will only intensify in the future. As the leading eccentric exponent, Britain cannot opt out.

What does such a foreign policy mean? How does it work in practice? Can it be implemented? Is it of any use? To answer these questions a distinction has to be drawn between strategy and tactics. As any chess player knows, to win you need both. Short term manoeuvring to gain this or that advantage on minor issues within the EU will of course never cease. They are the bread and butter of diplomacy and British leaders will, no doubt, go on doing their bit. Alignments within the EU will vary with the nature of the issues. Serious reform of the CAP, for example, is now unlikely since the new entrants, with agriculture-dependent economies, will line up with France. Subjects like fishing rights, the environment, regulations relating to the workplace, consumer protection, will each create a different dividing line within a continuing EU debate. Important as these issues are, the ad hoc alliances they produce, do not in themselves amount to a foreign policy. In the past British diplomatic effort in Europe has focused exclusively on disparate issues and superficial alignments. What is worse, it has moved without an overall plan, without a coherent set of guiding principles. All tactics, no strategy.

So what are the objectives that could form the basis of a British foreign policy in Europe?

- To help shape the European Union as a voluntary association of independent nation states, not as an evolving sovereign political entity.
- To forge long-term strategic alliances with nations whose political culture and instincts are closer to British ones. The Dutch, Swedes, Danes, Finns, Norwegians, Hungarians and Czechs, all fall naturally into this category.
- To cultivate ties with the smaller nations who are increasingly aware and resentful of the Franco-German domination.
- To establish a meaningful dialogue with an incoming German administration, to prepare the ground for a closer political co-operation after Schröder's demise. It will take but a few short years for German politicians to understand that the

French alliance is no longer in their country's best interest.

- To try and isolate France, whenever and wherever possible. For the next few decades the political philosophy and objectives of France and Britain are bound to be incompatible.
- To consistently oppose the concentric political establishments in their attempt to establish a powerful European central authority.
- To foster links with anti-integrationist forces throughout the continent, be they political parties, movements, or individuals.
- To educate the people of historically concentric societies, rather than their political leaders, in the virtues of eccentric government.
- To stem the tide of European legislation and put an end to the endless stream of prescriptive regulation emanating from Brussels.
- To encourage professional, educational and commercial bodies within nation states to create their own pan-European association, independent of Brussels bureaucracy.
- To reduce government at all European levels thus releasing a wealth of entrepreneurial energy that is alone capable of creating an economically vibrant continent.
- To begin the long process of repatriating decision-making powers lost to the Union.
- To strive for the leadership of Europe, not by clever political manoeuvring, but by setting an example of the kind of political life style the people of the continent admire, envy, even desire.

At first sight such a set of objectives may seem abstract, impractical, vastly ambitious and too far removed from the realities of current European politics. Not so. They have a direct bearing on the position taken by Britain in respect of the Euro, the proposed European constitution, the continuing movement towards greater integration, the competence of Brussels, the function of a European Parliament and just about every key issue touching the political development of the continent. If they seem far removed from what is actually taking place at every summit, it is because the European people have become accustomed to a daily diet of integration, transfer of powers to a central authority and steady diminution of national independence. If they seem vastly ambitious, it is because many people in this country have come to think of the concentric drive towards a Greater Europe as unstoppable. Perhaps fifteen, ten or even five years ago such prognostications may have been understandable. The situation has changed significantly since and it is continuing to change fast.

As integration fever gripped political establishments, an impression has been created that if the relentless timetable slipped, Europe's once a lifetime opportunity would be lost forever. One was always left to wonder why this frenetic pace? The political climate experienced in Europe over the last few years demonstrates precisely why the pace has had to be forced. The leaders of the Greater Europe agenda, being intent on securing their place in history, were wary of the public reaction once the practical consequences of the project became reality. And, judging by present discontents, they had every right to be concerned. In Germany the new currency has proved a huge disappointment. It is associated with hidden inflation, unemployment and economic stagnation. Even if it was only a contributory cause to the country's ills, the majority of the people consider the sacrifice of the powerful Mark to have been a great mistake. France was the first to brush aside the Growth and Stability Pact, the supposed safeguard of the untried currency with customary Gallic flourish. "My first duty is employment and not to solve accounting equations and do mathematical problems until some office or other in some country or other is satisfied" declared Jean-Pierre Raffarin, the French Prime Minister. Disputes as to the consequences of having destroyed the Stability Pact are still ongoing but it is already clear that France, true to form, will not be penalised.

Negative attitudes on the continent towards a centralised Europe extend far beyond an unpopular Euro. Brussels is widely perceived as undisciplined, corrupt, interfering, ineffective and power-hungry. The continuing accounting scandals, the enormous waste of financial resources, the unstoppable flow of petty, stifling regulations are all having a cumulative effect. An over-ambitious competition policy that is being regularly overturned by the courts, after causing considerable industrial damage, does not help. The ability of France to maintain its ban on British beef with impunity for many years in the face of EU rulings at the highest level and dismiss the Stability Pact out of hand, demonstrated the lack of ultimate authority at the heart of a "unified" continent. The Netherlands holders of the EU presidency, at the time or writing, identified an attack on Brussels red tape as one of the key objectives of their tenure. Their effort may not bring any great relief, but the fact that a country hitherto at the forefront of integration is having second thoughts is significant.

In Britain, these negatives unfortunately tend to harden into a general anti-European orientation. The rise of the United Kingdom Independence Party should serve as a wake up call to the whole of the British political class. On the continent, the very same perceptions tend to breed resentment towards politicians and parties that are engaged in politicising Europe. The advantage of concentric over eccentric government is the relative ease with which things may be accomplished without tiresome public input. The disadvantage is that the public reaction is not eliminated, merely deferred, to erupt with some ferocity later. Recent elections indicate that we have now reached the pre-eruption stage in the concentric cycle both in France and Germany. The French, on their own admission, had to choose in the final round of voting between a fascist and a crook as their President. The turnout was the lowest registered in the history of the Fifth Republic. In Germany Schröder barely scraped back into power, helped by floods in the East and anti-American rhetoric in the West. He lacks the authority to carry out the painful make-over Germany so desperately needs. For a leader-led people a weak government in troubled times is deeply damaging.

The days of powerful figures, the likes of Konrad Adenauer, de Gaulle, Schmidt, Mitterrand, Kohl, are gone. The legacy they left behind is a political structure and a tradition that the ordinary European does not respect, support, or trust. There is still a warm feeling all over the continent towards the idea of a European community but, as an electorate, they feel alienated from, and indifferent to, the entire political process. People enjoy the ease of doing business, the freedom to move and work across national borders. They do not much care for the additional layer of administration and have even less time for political institutions superimposed on the ones they have which are already suspect. There are also distinct signs that many nations are beginning to resent the domination of the Franco-German axis. Their undisguised fury over the high-handed dismissal of the Stability Pact is an important case in point. The high handed attitude of the French political establishment towards *lesser* states is likely to turn this resentment into hostility and hostility into opposition. When Chirac tells the lesser nations to keep quiet on Iraq and stop behaving like badly brought up *children*, when his Ambassador to the court of St. James refers to Israel as a *shitty little country*, it won't be long before France will start experiencing a well deserved backlash.

In framing her foreign policy, it is vital that Britain understands that in France she has an implacable and formidable foe. Whether this opposition is open or deeply disguised, whether it is publicly discussed or whispered in the corridors of power, whether it is suspended for tactical reasons from time to time, it will remain a key factor in any European equation for some time to come. France has been a junior partner in global alliances dominated by America and Britain for well nigh a century. In Europe she has been the undisputed leader for the last forty years. De Gaulle, perhaps the greatest nationalist leader of the 20th-century, was initially a Euro-sceptic. But by 1962 he is quoted as saying: "Europe is the way for France to become what she has ceased to be since Waterloo." The French political establishment realises full well, much better than most British politicians do, that Britain is the only serious rival for the leadership. With her language no longer pre-eminent and sensing her culture under threat, France will do everything within her power to maintain a hard earned primacy on the continent. Given the negotiating skills, the diplomatic track record and the self-belief of her political elite, it will be a daunting task to dislodge France from this particular saddle. Nevertheless, if Europe is to have a lasting communal future, this must be done. To wean away European nations from a centrist French domination has to be one of the key objectives of Britain's European Policy in the coming decade.

Given Britain's relationship with the US and the Commonwealth, such a foreign policy for Europe is the only one that makes any sense. For if nation states preserve their identity within a harmonious continent, Britain's unique position may be of great service to Europe, to America, to the whole Western World. She has then the chance of becoming a pivotal link in the complex of alliances on which the defence, prosperity and cultural cohesion of our civilised world ultimately rests.

One of the strangest contentions of the Euro lobby is the claim that Britain would gain political influence by joining the Euro zone and being at the heart of a politically integrated continent. Such influence that this country has rests not on possessing the Euro badge but on the quality of Britain's political culture, the endurance and pre-eminence of her political institutions, membership of the UN Security Council and G8, the special relationship with the US and the Commonwealth, on hosting the world's foremost financial centre, on possessing the most effective military force in Europe, on being a senior member of the EU and being the largest market for Europe's exports. This is perfectly well understood on the continent, if not at home. It is precisely why such pressure is exerted on Britain to join the Euro and partake fully in the integrationist move. It is a great shame that politicians in this country are the only ones in the world who do not realise that the European Union has a greater need of Britain than Britain has of the Union.

18

Reclaiming Europe

England has saved herself by her exertions, and will,
as I trust, save Europe by her example
William Pitt

Among the people of our continent, there is no longer general support for the Euro, no love for Brussels and no great yearning for a Greater Europe. Momentum still carries some projects towards their goal, but the forces that generated this momentum are on the defensive. This is the turning point in the brief history of the Union, the opportunity for Britain to formulate and put in place a new European *people's* agenda. If its principal items appear somewhat radical, it is because we have all become used to hearing their opposite. Where the agenda entails changes in existing clauses of the EU treaty, they will come not so much in the course of negotiations between opposing national politicians as through pressure exercised by the public and the media on political parties throughout the continent. What follows is a preliminary short list. It is not meant to be complete but it will do as a start:

- No European constitution. No European President. No Single European Foreign Policy. No European military body. No European police force.
- No further erosion of existing national veto powers.
- No formal legal authority to the EU's Charter of Fundamental Rights.
- The reversal of the on-going centrally directed process of standardisation. Adopting common standards should be the task of national parliaments or the voluntary act of trade and professional bodies, nationally or internationally, not the business of Brussels. If farmers or greengrocers wish to give a legal definition to the leek, or an organic orange, let them do so on their own initiative and at their own expense.
- The ending of attempts to harmonise taxation and financial regulations across the EU. *Creating a level playing field* is an attractive sporting metaphor, but it does nothing for a dynamic, competitive economy. Companies prefer to locate here primarily because of the ease of doing business. It is open to any country to emulate the UK if she so chooses. Harmonisation of any sort implies regulation and regulation of any sort stifles initiative and competition.
- The *gradual* elimination of all subsidies. In the end, some decades down the road, there should be no net national beneficiaries of the EU budget. Such a move alone would probably reduce by half the unseemly political haggles that are such a turn-off for the general public. It would also ensure that any country wishing to join the EU, does so because it is

willing and able to live within its confines and not in the expectation of juicy benefits.

- The severe curtailing of Brussels, its regulatory powers, its administrative machinery, its budget, its political influence. This all goes together. Cut one and you cut the others too. This would scotch directives like the one currently dreamt up by Anna Diamantopoulou, the EU social affairs commissioner, forcing the insurance industry to ignore factual differences between the life expectancy of men and women and so adding, in the name of *gender solidarity*, 15 per cent to the costs all round. It would also assist bodies like the Financial Service Authority and the Accounting Standards Board, who find the flood of EU financial legislation (14 new pieces of it are due to come into force by 2006) beyond their powers to implement.

- The remodeling of the financial accounting practices of the EU along lines practiced by the civil service in the UK or any of the Scandinavian countries where corruption, indiscipline and mal-administration are the exception rather than the rule. The European Court of Auditors refused to endorse the EU accounts (with a turnover of £66 billion) on the grounds that they could only vouch for a bare 10 per cent of its spending. The rest was riddled with errors and abuse and moneys just kept disappearing. The accounts have not been signed off for the last nine years.

- The reform of the European Parliament more in line with old continental traditions. In other words, a talking shop with no independent legislative or administrative powers. In its present state it is meant to bolster the democratic credentials of the Union rather than exercising effective control over Brussels. The election of its members raises feeble electoral interest and has more to do with domestic than European politics. This may appear an undemocratic step but parliaments can only contribute to the democratic process if they have ultimate decision-making powers. If the European Parliament is to have such powers this must be at the expense of national parliaments. From a democratic point of view, there is only one thing worse than having no parliament at all and that is having two, one competing with the other.

• The repatriation of those decision-making powers that are not absolutely essential to the maintaining of an effective single economic zone. The line between economics and politics may be difficult to draw. Having a grey area does not mean that this distinction is not valid or useful. The Health and Safety provisions in the Maastricht Treaty, for example, should have been clearly left within the province of national governments. In any case, the balance has shifted far too far towards the political dimension. There is a long way to go before it is redressed.

• The redefining of the role of specialist bodies, currently operating under the Commission's umbrella, operating in distinct areas like foreign relations, trade, finance, agriculture and so on. Instead of trying to reduce everything to the lowest common denominator, constructing mandatory formulae, the emphasis should be on research, exchange of information, technology and creative thinking. Technocrats, with some experience and expertise in their field, should be making the running, not politicians intent on image, spin and the semblance of unity. Governments should be encouraged but not compelled to modify their policies and wherever and whenever a general accord is established, European leaders would at least sing from the same hymn sheet, even if not with one voice.

• The relaunching of the Ecu, as a freely floating currency based on a basket of weighted European currencies, initially probably the Euro, Stirling, Danish Krone, Swedish Krone and the Swiss Franc. The new Ecu would be created by a consortium of banks without having to seek official endorsement by any government. Initially it would be purely a paper instrument used for bonds and in large-scale trading between companies. If it gains in popularity, its compass may extend to traveller cheques and other financial instruments. Eventually it may have its own notes and coins. It is not meant to compete with any of the existing currencies, replace them or undermine them. It is an eccentric currency making its own way without the backing and control of a central bank or any combination of governments. Its function is simply to provide a convenient alternative means of intra-national trade and travel, without the heavy political baggage of the Euro. Of course, should the Euro fail to take root, the new

Ecu could well serve as a safety net for countries reluctant to re-adopt their old, defunct currency.

- A moratorium of 10 years on Summits, Treaties named after sundry cities, any new EU legislation, regulations, directives and modifications thereof. The volume of rules currently in force extends to 86,000 pages. Europe badly needs a breathing space. The principal work of the Commission during this period should consist of abolishing, simplifying and diluting existing EU laws and regulations, consistently reducing red tape and trimming Union budgets.

Such an agenda is certain of a universally hostile reception from the dominant political classes on the continent, the Central European Bank, the European Parliament and the Brussels establishment. They have laboured hard over many years to develop the present set-up and have a huge vested interest in keeping it going. Their very mindset would make a serious, objective consideration of these proposals impossible. Fortunately this agenda is not addressed to any of them. It is meant as an appeal to public opinion in this country, to the British political leadership and to the people of the mainland continent who are disenchanted with an artificial political construct and distrustful of the politicians frantically engaged in erecting it.

This agenda is deeply pro European, profoundly in accord with what most ordinary people across the continent would like to happen. It is not a short-term fix cobbled together by heads of government. It is an altogether different strategy to bring together the nations of a continent, over the medium term, into a community that has cohesive lasting power. Some of the proposals, like those relating to a constitution or the retention of veto powers, have an immediate impact. Others, like the overhaul and downsizing of Brussels or the establishing of a user friendly Ecu, require time, effort and a great deal of informed public education. It is vital, however, that the set of objectives are seen as a whole, as a coherent, positive alternative to the piecemeal concentric process of dismantling the nation state.

This agenda, backed by decisive leadership steeped in the eccentric political culture, would change at once the focus of the European debate. Instead of arguing about how fast, how far to relinquish national independence, people both here and on the continent would discuss ways of enhancing a Europe of nation states. Instead of haggling over how to transfer more and more power to the EU, the question would be how best to encourage the continent to grow gradually and naturally into a potent, enduring political entity.

A massive enlargement of the EU is taking place right now with the grave matter of the status of nation states still unresolved. As the administration of this vast, still expanding, heterogeneous, semi-political entity becomes ever more cumbersome, there will be increasing pressure for the abolition of national vetoes. Indeed, Tony Blair has clearly signaled already his readiness to participate in the process. We can look forward to years of intense diplomatic activity, government spin, compromise, horse trading and ambiguous agreements which mean one thing in Europe and another nearer home. This is typical of how the EU works at present. Deals are made at a high level, new treaties are concluded on specific matters, one at a time with the wider ramifications left in abeyance. When these ramifications become apparent, they are simply presented as essential to the management of the EU. Politicians create the momentum, the momentum drives the politicians and the people are left behind. Until it is too late, that is. Just ask the Germans about the Euro.

Setting out unambiguously such a European agenda, would create political shock waves and bring in its wake the customary warnings, threats and lectures on Euro-scepticism, British aloofness, selfishness, insularity, and lack of team spirit. Such a reaction is inevitable. It is also to be welcomed. Both here and on the continent, the resulting polemic would help crystallize the underlying issues that beset the future direction of the European Union. Within such a polemic it may not be so easy to fudge the truth about ultimate power, independence and the political framework of a united continent. A concentric Greater Europe now and an eventual democratic Europe in the longer term, are not compatible.

In the context of domestic politics, the three main parties would have difficulties in subscribing to this agenda. As for their leaders, they will, of course, not endorse it, despite fervently and continuously affirming a commitment to a fully independent Britain, to a British participation in a genuinely democratic continent, to a thorough overhaul of the Brussels machinery, to decentralizing power. Established political parties will only be compelled to heed such an agenda by a people's movement across the political spectrum that draws support from the media and the population. It will take time for the momentum to build but there are encouraging signs of awakening forces not just in Britain but in Denmark, Sweden, Holland, Spain and Italy. Even some influential people in France and Germany are beginning to entertain serious doubts about the whole Greater Europe enterprise.

Indeed, so deep is the unease felt about the European project that there is a growing temptation in this country to leave the EU altogether. Way beyond the numbers who actually voted UKIP in the recent European elections, a sizeable portion of the electorate seriously doubt the value of the country's membership in an organization whose ethos is so alien to British social, economic and political traditions. People, on the whole, are thoroughly fed up with what transpires in the name Europe. They feel, with some justification, that they were misled by their leaders in the past and suspect even more the latest sales pitch by the Hain-Mandelson-Blair consortium. In the circumstances, it seems satisfyingly simple and inviting to opt out. Nevertheless, it would be a grave tactical error for Britain to break unilaterally her treaty obligations and leave the European Union. Why?

The enlarged Union, as currently constituted, is becoming increasingly unmanageable. She is drowning in her own bureaucratic excesses, the foundation of her currency is in ruins, the economies of major members are stagnant, her laws are not interpreted and implemented with any degree of uniformity, her finances are shambolic and her popularity is on the wane all over the continent. Irrespective of integrationist ambition, if the Union is not to fall apart, the practicalities of life on the ground will bring about a radical retrenchment, a complete overhaul. It is important for the future well being of Europe that, as the tide turns back towards nation states, Britain should be there to help guide the transformation into a gradual, orderly retreat. The descent of the continent into temporary chaos, following a total collapse of the EU, would damage British economic and political interests. Serious political turbulence on the continent never left Britain unaffected and uninvolved in the past and is even less likely to do so in the future. A unilateral withdrawal from the EU would alienate Britain's likeminded friends and allies in the struggle against integration who depend on Britain as a counterweight to the centrism of the Franco-German axis. It would abandon a French-led, destabilized Europe to the kind of concentric fate the continent experienced over the last two or three centuries.

For Britain to leave the EU on her own initiative at this juncture would be both unnecessary and unwise. As the proposed constitution demonstrates, the dominant issue in coming years will be the location of crucial decision-making powers: will they rest with the nation states or will they migrate to the centre. If Britain does not compromise and rejects the constitution, at least as far she is concerned the status quo prevails. It is likely that at least some of the other nations will act likewise or, at any rate, accept the dismantling of the Giscardian edifice. If a number, even a majority, of member states then persist in going down the federal route, adopting the Constitution, it is they who will have to withdraw from the Union and create their own political entity instead. In practical terms, the odds are against this becoming a reality, but the essential economic structure of a common economic Europe, with all its benefits, would survive in any case.

The death of the constitution would, more likely, mark the turning point in the tide of the Greater Europe project.

The current status quo in the balance of power between the nations and the EU is unsustainable. With enlargement, the difficulty of managing the Union will force areas of decision-making to be either centralized or firmly retained by the Member States. These forks in the mapping of Europe's future will provide Britain with the ideal ground to start the long-haul of reclaiming the ground lost to Brussels over the last two decades. This is exactly what the majority of the British people want.

A bold declaration of a well-defined British position, a positive stance in favour of a slowly evolving, people-friendly continent, should make diplomatic life a lot easier. No longer would British negotiators appear defensive, constantly on the back foot, apologetically trying to stem the concentric tide, opting lamely out of this or that independence-eroding clause. They would no longer be fighting a series of exhausting rearguard actions. Instead, they would be presenting a challenge to the community to take another line, to move in a different direction, to accept another vision for Europe.

It goes without saying that for such a policy to become meaningful, it requires leaders of courage, conviction and self-belief who have not yet given up the idea that Britain has a unique and valuable political contribution to make to Europe. They will need to be backed by a strong public opinion and for that to happen the British people, especially the younger generation, will have to re-discover the country's essential identity. They will have to become aware of what exactly is at stake.

Why should the people on the continent pay heed to the lonely British voice? Firstly, there is a new political climate. The heady days of the eighties and nineties, when an integrated Europe in the making was bathed in a glamorous, idealistic light, are over. In the second place, it was Britain who resisted most strongly this concentric drive and cautioned, time after time, against a hasty central political construction. Thirdly, the general population of the continent is no longer impressed by the political elite driving the integrationist agenda. Finally, continental people, as individuals, have always admired and envied the political lifestyle of Britain. They are not particularly impressed by the local food, by the country's infrastructure, the goods it produces, its transport facilities and services. But they certainly would love to take the stable kind of tolerant British democracy back home with them. A statement of intent would find a resonance and provide a rallying point for the forces resisting centralization throughout the continent. The opportunity to lead Europe, presented to Britain at the end of the war, was not lost, it has merely been deferred. It should not be missed the second time around.

19

A Good European

This above all: to thine own self be true,
And it must follow, as the night the day,
Thou canst not then be false to any man
Shakespeare
Hamlet

Whilst European political establishments are absorbed in the internal mechanics of their continent, the world is moving on at an exponential pace. Constantly evolving technologies, a growing output of legislation and regulations, and the increasing complexity of the human race, do have a crucial bearing on the future of the Union. The EU had its origins in a Common Market that was conceived as a protective regional trading block, conferring a competitive advantage on the insiders. With goods, moneys, services, people and information throughout the world moving more freely and increasingly faster, the formation of trading blocks may no longer follow strictly geographic patterns. The mass/value relationship of goods in transit is rapidly moving in the direction of value, thus making physical distances less and less of a factor. Tariff barriers are coming down and money is moving from one computer terminal to another. The very concept of different currencies may itself disappear in the not too distant future. If nation states have finite lives, regional power blocks have them too, and theirs may be somewhat shorter.

Over the last four decades there has been an unparalleled growth in legislation of all sorts and from all quarters. Red tape, be it domestic, European or global, threatens to stifle the rapidly diminishing individual scope of action in every sphere. In law, man is overprotected, over regulated, over administered. In practice, human beings are no more free of danger, accident, violence, exploitation and negligence than they have ever been. World resources spent on cultivating law, generating litigation, multiplying lawyers and layers of courts, have reached proportions ever harder to justify. The law of diminishing returns has long been exceeded. It is axiomatic that European integration will keep producing a stream of new legislation and a tide of new regulations over and above the flow that is drowning enterprise and traditional life here already. The British people simply cannot afford any additional layers of administration, duplication of overlapping authorities and never ending paper work that invades every nook and cranny of their everyday lives.

It is increasingly difficult to predict, much less control, global patterns of human evolution and behaviour. The world can do little about the potentially devastating effect of unchecked population growth. The end of the cold war, the dramatic collapse of a communist empire, was not so easily foreseen. The rise of a militant Islam and the emergence of organised terrorism on the current scale, found world leaders unprepared. What comes next?

Nobody knows. The human race has become so complex that its future is more a matter of imaginative speculation than rational analysis. In a world of such uncertainties, it is critical that a country should be able to react to any major unexpected event with speed, unity and strength. For that to happen, the government and the people have to be in instinctive accord, flexible in approach and with full freedom for incisive action. Recent events in the international arena demonstrated, if such a demonstration was needed, that the European Union is a world away from being able to react fast, cohesively and effectively in a crisis. Therefore, it is essential for Britain, now more than ever, to retain her freedom for independent action.

These in themselves are reasons enough to jealously guard British independence but when they are reinforced by the more specific drawbacks of the Euro and profound concerns raised by the proposed constitution, the case against European integration is overwhelming. And yet, according to a recent survey, although there was a majority of 3 to 1 for keeping the Pound, over half the people questioned thought that Britain would join the Euro anyway. This is a frightening statistic for it demonstrates the extent to which the population is resigned to the idea that integration is inevitable. It is this general sense of individual helplessness that allowed Kohl to persuade Germany to sacrifice the Mark and it is what Tony Blair counts on to get Britain into the Euro. In the run-up to a referendum, whether on the Constitution or the Euro, an alliance of a committed Labour government, Conservative Europhiles, federalist Liberal Democrats and influential Trade Union leaders will hammer home a single message: Britain must be part of an integrated Europe, there is no choice.

Yet of the many claims in favour of integration, the one based on its inevitability is the weakest one. Virtually all historic events appear inevitable in hindsight. Yet most historic events, claimed as inevitable before their occurrence, have never come to pass at all. The Marxist dogma is founded on the historical inevitability of a world revolution resulting in the dictatorship of the working classes. For a good hundred years the communist advance seemed unstoppable. To almost everyone outside this island, and to many people within it, a German victory in 1940 appeared a foregone conclusion. The power of the Trade Unions seemed unbreakable, until Margaret Thatcher came along. For the children of the 20th-century, rising inflation has been an ineluctable fact of economic life, but is that still the case today?

The classic argument based on inevitability is simplistic. It takes as its starting point a clearly observable trend, then draws a linear extension of it into the future and concludes that such a development is historically "inevitable". Such a perception may become a self-fulfilling prophecy and therein lies its greatest threat. Over the last forty years the countries of Europe have undoubtedly come closer together. The nation states have given up some rights of independent action. Some common institutions have taken over the functions of national ones. Does it follow that European countries are bound to come ever closer together? That more and more national rights will be given up? That common institutions will increasingly take over the function of national ones? That this process is inevitable? The integrationist movement would certainly like it to be so, but reality seldom works like this. Trends do not have an infinite life, their patterns are generally not simply linear, and, more often than not, they create their own counter-trends.

To reinforce and exploit the perception of "inevitability", the integrationists like to employ an image of some sort of vehicle, a bus, a boat, a train that is moving inexorably forward at some speed. Any hesitation or delay by the British conjures up a horrifying picture of them missing out on a wonderful voyage. (It is advisable, by the way, to pay particular attention to the word *forward*, a word most favoured by politicians when they have nothing specific to say. The frequency of its use is directly proportional to the vacuity of their message.) If anything is inevitable, it is not Britain joining the Euro but the ultimate failure of a single European currency in the absence of a fully integrated European state. And the likelihood of such a state, in our lifetime, is diminishing year by year.

It has become fashionable in some quarters, both here and on the continent, to reproach the British for not being European enough. It is a curious reproach, especially in the mouth of leaders whose countries owe, in part, their independence to Britain. A good European is not easily defined. To aspire to this denomination, some integrationists believe, Britain should go with the continental drift, with whatever the dominant political establishment in Europe has in mind. In that case, the British would have been better Europeans if they had let Napoleon have his way, or made peace with Hitler in 1940, or excluded the continent from the protective NATO umbrella. Perhaps this is why the only acknowledgment Britain has ever received for saving Europe from being a German continent, is an annual Christmas tree gifted by

Norway. But then Norway is not, as it so happens, part of the European Union.

Perhaps being a good European means surrendering important national interests. For France this would amount to allowing the Common Agricultural Policy to be radically reformed and the relocation of the European Parliament from Strasbourg; for Spain, abandoning the claim to Gibraltar and the right to fish around British coasts; for Ireland, Portugal and Greece, foregoing the benefits of regional subsidies, and so on. No major concessions of national interests seem to have been forthcoming from any EU members thus far. On the contrary, each and every European leader strives to protect and enhance the national interest of his own country and is judged by his constituency accordingly. Tony Blair himself makes a great play on his commitment to defend British national interest above all else.

Then again, being a good European may translate into conformity to Brussels directives and compliance with EU rules. On such an official league table, France, unsurprisingly, is by far the worst offender whilst Britain comes somewhere in the middle. Unofficially, everyone knows that there are two ways of complying with European rules and regulations: the stricter way, as practiced in Sweden, Denmark, Holland, Germany, Britain and Finland and the Mediterranean way. France is a special case, she continues as she has always done: she practices what is beneficial for her and disregards what is not.

If being a good European is measured by contributions made in respect of the rights and liberties of the individual citizen, the British must easily outrank all other nations. Religious, racial and political tolerance, freedom of speech, protection and equality in law, parliamentary democracy itself, were established here decades, if not centuries before they have come to be accepted as European ideals.

In the integrationist vocabulary, a good European is one who is prepared to throw his business habits, his laws, his political institutions and traditions into one huge European melting pot to adopt newly emerging common forms and patterns, whatever they be. In terms of such a definition the British are bad, very bad, Europeans, and are likely to remain so. For what Britain stands to lose is a great deal more than any other European nation and what she is likely to gain is highly questionable at best, calamitous at worst.

The debate about the Euro, a European constitution, about Britain's relationship with the continent, is bound to keep generating confusion of every conceivable kind. This debate should not be about Britain leaving the EU, about being anti-European, about the convenience of taking holiday cash, about fluctuating exchange rates, about exactly how far Europe extends, about the precise powers of a future European president, about the wording of a pan-European constitution. The essence of this debate is about the kind of Britain people in this country want to have as their future home.

The Euro is not an economic but a political currency. Joining the Euro is not an economic necessity, it is a pledge of political commitment to partake in a process that leads ultimately to total European integration. The motivation and drive towards integration emanates from European political establishments. The unification of the continent is not inspired by the spontaneous yearning of its people. A future Federal European State is yet another grandiose vision dreamt up in the political culture and intellectual climate of a continent whose history is littered with the ruins of precisely such visions.

Having a currency, a written constitution, a parliament and a political president do not, in themselves, amount to an enduring political state. These trappings of power are no substitute for a single nation living within well defined boundaries. The magnificent achievements of what may be termed *European culture*, in the fields of Philosophy, Music, Law, Language, Literature, Art and Architecture, have their roots in individual societies with a sense of self-identity. To preserve the creative sources and cross-fertilisation of cultures it is vital not to merge the European nations into a standardised, politically homogenised state. A nation, a people, cannot be cobbled together in a matter of decades. The aftermath of Versailles and the post-colonial constructs in the third world should have taught us that much. This particular enterprise, without a strong, natural centre of power, will founder on the deeply ingrained national differences in character, culture, habit and attitude right across Europe. The political edifice presently under construction, in its ambition, scope and dimension, will render any kind of European Union ungovernable.

After all is said and done, the British people have a stark choice to make. They can do nothing and drift along with the continental current or fight to preserve their eccentric, national identity. They can vote to join the Euro, allow a written European constitution to be imposed on them, forego their vetoes, let control slip to Brussels and throw in their lot with a concentric majority. It is, in the short term, the easier option. It takes no effort, avoids confrontation, abrogates responsibility. To stand firm against a countervailing trend, to rely on one's own resources, to stick to principles, is much harder. It requires courage and self-belief. This is true of individuals as it is of nations.

It is as yet uncertain when a referendum on the Euro will be held. It is probable that one on a European Constitution will precede it. There is even a danger that no referenda of any kind will be on offer, at least in Britain, until the process of integration had gone far enough to make any consultation of the people meaningless. On the continent, decisions reached between political leaders at various summits are almost invariably endorsed or ratified by national parliaments with the general public left out of the equation. So the momentum builds and a new kind of political entity is being negotiated into existence in the artificial hothouses of international diplomacy without too many people being involved. This has ever been the way of life in concentric cultures, cultures that leave the ordinary man with a feeling that he has no say, that he does not matter, that he has no choice except to strike, to block roads, to mount barricades.

Thus far, politics in Britain has not worked like this. The independence of the country and the right of the people to be governed by consent, have been inviolate. Creeping continental integration poses a threat to both. In a recent speech in Cardiff, the Prime Minister set out his agenda: strengthening the central authority of Brussels, removing systematically national vetoes, establishing a permanent European presidential structure, enlarging common European institutions and increasing the scope of common European policies. He also said, by the way, that he wanted a Europe of sovereign nations. This is the kind of cynical double-speak that makes ordinary people despair of politics.

The people of this country will have to find their voice and make damn sure this voice is strong enough to command the attention of politicians tempted to negotiate by subtle degrees Britain off the map altogether. For what it's worth, I personally believe that the British will resist any further erosion of their decision-making powers. I believe that they will vote to keep the Pound, they will not just swallow a European constitution and they will struggle hard against any further surrender of the national veto. I believe that integrationist political leaders within all three parties, and the Brussels club, have seriously misjudged the mood of the country and the character of the people, something all too easily done in the frenzy of ongoing summitry. Political culture here is just too strongly based on non-conformism, on individual self-reliance, on grass-root democracy, on anti-authoritarian instinct, to be otherwise. If 31 small parish councils can combine on their own to effectively influence the traffic management of the A35, if a huge Countryside Alliance can spring up from nowhere, if government continues to live in fear of the popular press, then people of this country will surely not let go of their own identity. An easygoing environment, fluid and flexible structures, personal freedom and belief in the individual, are what made this nation great. If they have been helpful to the country in the past, these attributes are now critical for her survival.

If Britain is able to unite her people around the anti-integrationist principle, and adhere to it, she will be at the heart of the continent as the Greater Europe project falls apart. Beyond the Danes and Swedes, other European